The American Evangelical Story

The American Evangelical Story

A History of the Movement

Douglas A. Sweeney

Baker Academic

Grand Rapids, Michigan

© 2005 by Douglas A. Sweeney

Published by Baker Academic
a division of Baker Publishing Group
P.O. Box 6287, Grand Rapids, MI 49516-6287
www.bakeracademic.com

Printed in the United States of America

Library of Congress Cataloging-in-Publication Data
Sweeney, Douglas A.
    The American evangelical story : a history of the movement / Douglas A. Sweeney.
        p.   cm.
    Includes bibliographical references and index.
    ISBN 0-8010-2658-X
    1. Evangelicalism—United States—History. 2. United States—Church history. I. Title
    BR1642.U5S94 2005
    277.3′082—dc22   2004029538

To
my parents,
Mark and Janet Sweeney,
in gratitude for my evangelical heritage

Contents

Preface

Roughly one out of every ten people in the world is an evangelical. So say the number crunchers who keep the closest tabs on the global church. By the first year of the twenty-first century, the world population had topped six billion. Over two billion people identified themselves with Christianity. Of these, well over half a billion were "evangelical" Christians.

Of course, estimating the size of Christian groups is difficult. Hard numbers are hard to come by, and different groups report membership differently. Further, the leading authority on the statistical growth of the church around the world (Professor David Barrett of Regent University) is occasionally criticized for the generosity of his figures. Nonetheless, Barrett suggests that if Pentecostals and charismatics are counted as evangelicals—and as we will see later, I think they should be—then there are four-fifths of a billion evangelicals today. Pentecostals and charismatics alone total 570 million. The number of other evangelicals exceeds 242 million.[1]

A century ago, the number of Christians *of any kind* was smaller than this, and the vast majority of the world's Christians lived in Europe and North America. But the twentieth century witnessed a virtual explosion of evangelicalism, a blast that rocked the two-thirds world more powerfully than the West. Indeed, by the early 1970s, most Christians lived *outside* the West, a result of evangelical growth that has shifted the church's center of gravity. Today, less than 40 percent of Christians live in Europe and North America. In fact, the church is growing faster now on the continent of Africa than it has *ever* grown *anywhere* before.[2]

As we will see in the pages that follow, the evangelical movement (of which I count myself a part) emerged less than three hundred years ago as a focused initiative for the renewal of Protestant Europe's state churches. But over the course of its brief history, it has literally changed the face of the world. Today, Protestants, Roman Catholics, and Eastern Orthodox participate—men and women, rich and poor, people of color more often than not.

This book describes how this came to be—not by attempting to chart evangelical history *everywhere* in the world but by focusing narrowly on what has been its most prodigious global center. Even now, non-Western evangelicals are developing the resources they will need to take the reins of this global movement. They already provide the lion's share of its full-time ministry leaders. They will soon command the attention of the mainstream scholarly world as well. Indeed, the cutting edge of scholarship in the field of Christian history is already in the church in Africa, Asia, and Latin America. But sadly, this is a recent trend, and as an American historian, I am not well trained to write such history. So I offer the following *not* as the be-all and end-all of the story but as a survey of the role of U.S. Americans[3] in its plot.

After providing a summary of recent debates concerning the scope of evangelicalism, I tell the story of its birth in the transatlantic Great Awakening[4] and its development in the United States through many cultural changes and challenges. Along the way, I try to account for the broad range of individuals, institutions, issues, and doctrines that have made us who we are. I offer this book, then, as an *introduction* to evangelicalism for Christians interested in the historical roots of its recent, massive growth. Recognizing that it will be used primarily in colleges and seminaries, I have filled it with the kinds of information needed by students seeking a detailed understanding of Christian history. But I have also tried to avoid the sins of the worst scholarly texts. To the best of my ability, and with the advice of pastors and others better attuned to popular tastes, I have recounted what I take to be a fascinating story in a concise and readable manner—hoping to gain a wider hearing for the evangelical past. At the end of each chapter, I offer suggestions for further reading. I have also made some pointed claims about evangelicalism that I hope will edify readers not *required* to study this book! Throughout its pages, I try to show that though we have always been diverse, and though we have never proved morally blameless, evangelicals share a heritage that is both rich and spiritually powerful—a legacy worth passing on to future generations.

In Joshua 4:21–24, we read that when Israel crossed the Jordan to inhabit the Promised Land, they built a memorial to God's faithfulness out of twelve stones from the riverbed. After setting them up at Gilgal, Joshua declared to the people of God:

> In the future when your descendants ask their fathers, "What do these stones mean?" tell them, "Israel crossed the Jordan on dry ground." For the Lord your God dried up the Jordan before you until you had crossed over. The Lord your God did to the Jordan just what he had done to the Red Sea when he dried it up before us until we had crossed over. He did this so that all the peoples of the earth might know that the hand of the Lord is powerful and so that you might always fear the Lord your God.[5]

My hope and prayer for the chapters that follow is that they too might be a memorial, a compilation of stones selected from the riverbed of *our* history that testify to God's faithfulness among us.

Let me be perfectly clear. America's evangelicals are *not* the Lord's New Israel—God's chosen people or favored nation—despite the arrogant claims of some of our founding fathers. But we *have* proved just as wayward as ancient Israel tended to be, and yet God has managed to spread the gospel through our movement. In fact, it might be said that evangelicals epitomize the message of Paul in the first chapter of 1 Corinthians:

> Brothers, think of what you were when you were called. Not many of you were wise by human standards; not many were influential; not many were of noble birth. But God chose the foolish things of the world to shame the wise; God chose the weak things of the world to shame the strong. He chose the lowly things of this world and the despised things—and the things that are not—to nullify the things that are, so that no one may boast before him.

11

It is because of him that you are in Christ Jesus, who has become for us wisdom from God—that is, our righteousness, holiness and redemption. Therefore, as it is written: "Let him who boasts boast in the Lord."

verses 26–31

As this book will amply demonstrate, evangelicals have nothing to brag about "save in the death of Christ our God" (as one of our early hymn writers put it). But God has used us in a manner unique in all of Christian history. Our story, therefore, is a narrative of "the surprising work of God," a song of "amazing grace . . . that saved a wretch like me." Won't you pray that God will use it not to puff evangelical pride but so that "the peoples of the earth might know that the hand of the LORD is powerful and so that you might always fear the LORD your God"?

Acknowledgments

Scores of people and institutions have contributed to this book. Thanks go first to Robert N. Hosack, my acquisitions editor at Baker Academic, who solicited the work and waited patiently as I wrote it. Thanks go next to my students at Trinity, who represent the future of the evangelical movement. I count it a privilege to serve them. They teach me new things every day about the evangelical world, deepening my reflection on its nature and history. More importantly, their passionate commitment to the gospel inspires confidence in (and eager anticipation of) things to come.

Numerous colleagues perused parts of this book in manuscript form and/or offered sage advice about its contents. Thanks especially to the following for lending valuable expertise: Don Carson, Peter Cha, Gaston Espinosa, Brad Gundlach, David Kling, Mark Noll, Bob Priest, David Roebuck, Janet Sweeney, Mark Sweeney, Joe Thomas, John Wigger, John Woodbridge, and Bob Yarbrough. Rick Cook and Scott Manetsch read the entire manuscript, making suggestions for improvement along the way (true friends indeed). I am also blessed by association with three regional dialogue groups, each of which offered insights that helped to shape this work: the "Common Root" evangelical–Roman Catholic dialogue (especially Tom Baima and Kevin Vanhoozer); Chicago's evangelical seminar on race and ethnicity, funded generously by the Wabash Center and Weyerhaeuser

Foundation (especially Hank Allen, Peter Cha, Al Nieves, Bob Priest, and Kersten Priest); and the interdepartmental group of Trinity's new Center for Theological Understanding (especially Steve Greggo, Brian Maier, David Pao, Bob Priest, Eckhard Schnabel, Kevin Vanhoozer, Bob Yarbrough, and Lawson Younger). Onalee Pierce, my graduate fellow, contributed timely fact checking and bibliographical research. Sharon Ralston of Fuller Seminary's McAlister Library offered valuable assistance from Pasadena. For help with pictures, I thank Hayden Thornburg, Chris Armstrong, Steven Gertz, Mary Ann Jeffrey, Doreen Fast, Wayne Weber, Rob Krapohl, and Ken Minkema.

Several academic and church groups invited me to test the ideas conveyed below. On the academic front, my thanks go to Gordon-Conwell Theological Seminary in Charlotte, North Carolina, for inviting me to speak about America's evangelicals in class and convocation during the fall of 2000 (special thanks to David Wells, Steve Klipowicz, and Garth Rosell). Thanks as well to the fine scholars in the Southwest Region of the Evangelical Theological Society who invited me to give their plenary lectures in 2001 (especially Andy Woodring, Doug Blount, and the LeTourneau College faculty).

On the ecclesiastical front, I should thank the many churches that put up with my rehearsals of the history of evangelicals: First Lutheran Church of Nashville (especially Pastor Alan Watt); Bethesda Lutheran Church, New Haven (especially Pastor Michael Merkel); St. Paul Lutheran Church, Waukegan, Illinois (especially Pastor Carol Wasemiller); St. Mark Lutheran Church, Lindenhurst, Illinois (especially Pastor Terry Breum); Moody Church, Chicago (especially pastors Erwin Lutzer, Steve Mason, Bill Bertsche, and Mark Pirrie); Arlington Heights Evangelical Free Church, Arlington Heights, Illinois; Lancaster Evangelical Free Church, Lancaster, California (especially Pastor Daniel Holmquist); Winnetka Bible Church, Winnetka, Illinois; Christ Church, Lake Forest, Illinois (especially Pastor Mike Woodruff); Crossroads Church, Grayslake, Illinois (especially Pastor Steve Farish); and Western Springs Baptist Church, Western Springs, Illinois.

Finally, important family members have supported this work immeasurably. My wife, Wilma, and son, David, fill our home with love and joy. My in-laws, Homer (Hommo) and Tena (Trientje) Hamster, have taught me more than they will ever know about America's evangelicals—especially about their singularly American characteristics. My parents, to whom I dedicate this book with love and respect, have taught me not only what it means to be an American evangelical but also what it means to persevere with faith, courage, and remarkable integrity when other evangelicals disappoint us.

1

Evangelical

What's in a Word?

> Then Jesus came to them and said, "All authority in heaven and
> on earth has been given to me. Therefore go and make disciples
> of all nations, baptizing them in the name of the Father and of the
> Son and of the Holy Spirit, and teaching them to obey everything
> I have commanded you. And surely I am with you always, to the
> very end of the age."
>
> Matthew 28:18–20

Evangelicals are gospel people. On this nearly all agree. We are
people of the Great Commission found in the Scripture text
above. Indeed, the English word *evangelical* comes from the
Greek word *euangelion*—meaning "gospel" or, more literally,
"good news" or "glad tidings" (as in, "I bring you *good news* of
great joy that will be for all the people" [Luke 2:10]). As Timothy George defined us in *Christianity Today*, "Evangelicals are
a worldwide family of Bible-believing Christians committed to
sharing with everyone everywhere the transforming good news

of new life in Jesus Christ, an utterly free gift that comes through faith alone in the crucified and risen Savior."[1]

But beyond this basic definition, precious little consensus exists among those who have tried to describe the evangelical movement. What's more, there are plenty of Christians, past and present, here and abroad, who have described themselves in this way without claiming the "evangelical" label. So what does it mean, exactly, to be an evangelical Christian? What is unique about the evangelical movement?

Various evangelical leaders have sought to give answers to these questions, though the questions themselves are now so contested that no single answer will satisfy all. Among theologians, the best-known answer comes from Alister McGrath. In his book titled *Evangelicalism and the Future of Christianity*, McGrath suggests that "evangelicalism is grounded on a cluster of six controlling convictions, each of which is regarded as being true, of vital importance and grounded in Scripture. . . . These six fundamental convictions can be set out as follows:

1. The supreme authority of Scripture as a source of knowledge of God and a guide to Christian living.
2. The majesty of Jesus Christ, both as incarnate God and Lord and as the Savior of sinful humanity.
3. The lordship of the Holy Spirit.
4. The need for personal conversion.
5. The priority of evangelism for both individual Christians and the church as a whole.
6. The importance of the Christian community for spiritual nourishment, fellowship and growth."[2]

Among historians, David Bebbington's definition is best known, though it features four rather than six evangelical characteristics. In his widely used book titled *Evangelicalism in Modern Britain*, Bebbington writes that "there are . . . four qualities that have been the special marks of Evangelical religion: *conversionism*, the belief that lives need to be changed; *activism*, the expression of the gospel in effort; *biblicism*, a particular regard for the Bible; and what may be called *crucicentrism*, a stress on the sacrifice of Christ on the cross. Together they form a quadrilateral of priorities that is the basis of Evangelicalism."[3]

Both of these scholars admit that there is more to evangelicals than one can express in such definitions, but neither is very keen on defining the movement any further. As a result, the leading commentators on evangelicalism today seldom move beyond the kind of definition provided by Timothy George. Indeed, some critics complain that these definitions are *lacking in definition*, causing confusion and even resentment among nonspecialists. Such critics point out that *most* Christians have tended to define their faith in these ways, whether or not they have thought of themselves as evangelicals. Others contend more strongly that self-professing evangelicals have actually commandeered this label, ignoring its use by groups that predate their movement by centuries. (This argument usually comes from confessional Lutherans, though it could be—and has been—made just as strongly by other gospel-centered groups, some of which were using the label before the evangelical *movement* existed.)

Such claims leave most of the rest of us scratching our weary heads, wondering if evangelicalism means anything more than conservative Christianity—no matter what make or model— whether it distinguishes its adherents from anything more than Christian liberalism. Has this movement grown so successful over the course of the previous century that its leaders no longer see it as being at odds with the rest of the church? Is evangelicalism just a synonym for what is now mainstream Christian faith? In short, has the evangelical movement lost its saltiness?

Part of the challenge that anyone faces in trying to define the movement more narrowly has to do with the great wealth of evangelical diversity. Any movement as immense as that of global evangelicalism will include many who share little else in common. Men and women on every continent count themselves as evangelicals, from the very rich to the very poor, from the well educated to the uneducated, both capitalists and socialists, democrats, monarchians, and everything in between.

Not only do evangelicals come in different shapes and sizes, but they also participate in hundreds of different denominations—some of which were founded in opposition to some of the others! The vast majority are Protestant, but even among the Protestants there are Lutheran, Reformed, and Anabaptist evangelicals. There are Anglicans, Methodists, Holiness people, and Pentecostals. There are Calvinists and Arminians.[4] Some evangelicals go to churches that are overseen by bishops, others by presbyteries, while most prove fiercely independent. Some adhere to historic confessions drafted in Augsburg and Westminster. Still others oppose the use of confessions altogether.

There has never been—and there never will be—an evangelical denomination, despite the references one hears to the evangelical church. We have no evangelical constitution, no formal guidelines for faith and practice. Though there are plenty of famous leaders and institutions around which we rally (Billy Graham, *Christianity Today*, the World Evangelical Alliance, etc.), none of these has final authority in shaping the evangelical movement. We have no card-carrying membership, not even an official membership list. Distinguishing "insiders" from "outsiders" can prove to be tricky business. The faith and practice of many self-described evangelicals are deemed marginal or even entirely unacceptable to the majority of evangelicals. At the same time, many exist who fit the bill remarkably well but whose participation in the movement is only marginal. (For reasons that will be discussed later, many African American Christians fall into this latter category.)

In short, when viewed from the perspective of our multiplicity, we evangelicals hold hardly anything in common. We are a people more remarkable for our differences than our union. This has led some to depict evangelicals largely in terms of diversity, explaining the movement by means of taxonomies of various evangelical species. The taxonomies of Robert Webber are perhaps the best known, for he has mapped out no fewer than *sixteen* evangelical species—in the United States alone! Webber lists fundamentalist, dispensational, and conservative evangelicals; Anabaptist, Wesleyan, and charismatic evangelicals; black, progressive, and even radical evangelicals.[5] His list goes on, but his point is already well taken. Evangelicals are extremely diverse. Our constituency is comprised of innumerable subgroups, each with its own major emphases, institutions, and even leaders. Any attempt to describe the movement must come to terms with this reality.

Consequently, even the best of present-day evangelical scholars tend to oscillate between weak-willed efforts to define the movement clearly (as seen above), more creative attempts to depict it not propositionally but metaphorically, and frustratingly fuzzy assurances that we share a general "family resemblance" (i.e., I can't define evangelicals, but I know one when I see one).

The late historian Timothy Smith spent much of his long and prolific career coloring in what he liked to call the "evangelical mosaic," a metaphor Smith used to honor the individuality of his subjects while denoting the beauty of the movement when viewed as a whole. Late in his life, Smith turned his attention to a different metaphor, applying his colors to a more dynamic "evangelical kaleidoscope." Whereas a mosaic is a single, static, and permanent piece of art, a kaleidoscope allows for many colorful combinations, it is much more accessible than a mosaic, and it also depicts the dynamism of the evangelical movement.[6]

Another historian, Randall Balmer, prefers to refer to evangelicalism as a "patchwork quilt," a metaphor better suited to signify "folk art rather than fine art" (Balmer describes evangelicalism as "America's folk religion," by which he means that it is the faith of America's common people) and to exemplify what in Balmer's view is "the absence of an overall pattern" to the movement. In his book and **PBS** series, *Mine Eyes Have Seen the Glory: A Journey into the Evangelical Subculture in America*, Balmer depicts the movement by means of a series of brief, folksy vignettes that, taken together, impress viewers with their rich variety more than their unity. Balmer has stitched them all together, but it is difficult to tell whether his patches share anything other than this in common.[7]

A growing number of other pundits has chosen to cease with definitions, claiming that evangelicals defy a neat and tidy categorization. In a landmark study tellingly titled *The Variety of American Evangelicalism*, Donald Dayton and Robert Johnston have led the way. Johnston responds to the "definitional impasse" concerning American evangelicalism with the suggestion that evangelicals resemble a large, extended family and should be described in only a general manner in terms of their "family resemblance" rather than pigeonholed with excessive, propositional precision.[8]

Dayton is the most radical of all the evangelical commentators. He has called for a "moratorium" on the label "evangelical," which he rejects as "theologically incoherent, sociologically confusing, and ecumenically harmful."[9] It is theologically incoherent, in Dayton's estimation, because evangelical theologians are always at war with one another and have never united around a common doctrinal platform. It is sociologically confusing because it obscures more than it reveals about most of the groups who are so labeled. It is ecumenically harmful because the leading definers of the movement represent what Dayton calls a myopic, rather elitist, even bourgeois "Presbyterian" model of evangelical history.

This latter point is the one to which Dayton has devoted the bulk of his time. It is also the one that requires the most unpacking. In Dayton's view, the very scholars who spill the most ink on evangelicalism are responsible for misleading us as to its nature and significance. Indeed, they have focused mainly in their writings on the movement's intellectual leaders, usually privileged white men with Calvinistic worldviews and cultural pretensions that put them at odds with the vast majority of their followers (i.e., men such as Jonathan Edwards, Charles Hodge, and Carl F. H. Henry). According to Dayton, however, most *real* or *everyday* evangelical Christians hardly ever fit this description. White men are in the minority, few evangelicals are intellectuals, and evangelical beliefs seldom conform to a standard Calvinistic worldview. In fact, a simple head count of evangelicals, both here and around the world, reveals that most of us hail from lower-class, "Pentecostal" religious traditions (a blanket term Dayton uses in opposition to "Presbyterian" and that refers broadly to Arminian, Wesleyan, Holiness, and/or Pentecostal Christians, people who rarely resonate with the words of Calvinist intellectuals).

This is not the place to flesh out the rest of Dayton's argument. Suffice it to say that he is so taken by the extent of evangelical diversity (especially at the grass roots) and so concerned to avoid co-optation by Calvinist elites that he has called evangelicals to stop employing "evangelical" as a label, and he resists attempts to define this outmoded term.

Even Dayton's arch-nemesis, the well-known historian George Marsden, has been affected by this critique—despite his own evangelical Calvinism. Marsden is arguably the most proficient scholar of evangelicalism today. He has spent his life explaining the movement and trying to give it some definition. At times, however, and especially as Dayton's views have gained support, even Marsden has thrown in the towel and said—perhaps with tongue in cheek—that an evangelical is simply someone who admires Billy Graham!

All of this skepticism and infighting leaves hard-driving Calvinists such as Michael Horton and D. G. Hart complaining, in Horton's words, that "quarrels over the evangelical trademark are probably a profound waste of time and precious energy," or in Hart's, that "evangelicalism needs to be relinquished as a religious identity because it does not exist."[10] Horton and Hart, like many other erstwhile evangelical leaders, appear more interested today in reinforcing their fellow Calvinists than in working on cooperative ventures with other so-called evangelicals. And who can blame them, given the endless and usually fruitless disputations over evangelical identity? If we evangelicals have so much trouble even deciding who we are, then how will we ever work together *as evangelicals*? If we encourage one another to wallow contented in our diversity, won't large-scale evangelical ventures prove even more futile in years to come?

Such frustration is understandable and hardly unique these days. But is this really where we are left as we enter the church's third millennium? Of course, if I thought so I would not be writing this book on the movement's nature and history. More importantly, I would not devote so much time to evangelical ministries.

I believe there is still such a thing as a definite and definable evangelical movement today. In fact, in my view, it is the most vital Christian movement on the scene. I will be the first to confess that we evangelicals are rich in all sorts of diversity. What's more, in this multicultural age, we are learning (by God's grace) to celebrate our diversity. But I do not think we are left with only endless differences. In fact, we evangelicals together hold much that is precious *across* our cultural boundaries. We share a legacy brimming over with common principles and practices. We have always made good on this rich legacy in a wide variety of ways, but we have made good on a *common legacy* nonetheless.

Let me conclude this chapter by taking a shot at my own definition, one that I think summarizes the best of our common evangelical legacy and sets the stage for the story that follows: Evangelicals comprise a movement that is rooted in classical Christian orthodoxy, shaped by a largely Protestant understanding of the gospel, and distinguished from other such movements by an eighteenth-century twist. Or put more simply (though less precisely), evangelicals are a movement of orthodox Protestants with an eighteenth-century twist. We are certainly not the only authentic Christians in the world, nor are we the only ones to whom the term *evangelical* applies. But we are unique in our commitment to gospel witness around the world. Our uniqueness is best defined by our adherence to: (1) beliefs most clearly stated during the Protestant Reformation and (2) practices shaped by the revivals of the so-called Great Awakening.

Of course, the rest of this book is devoted to fleshing out this definition, but a brief word is in order here about a few of its key terms: *movement, orthodox Protestants,* and *eighteenth-century twist.*

First, evangelicals comprise a *movement,* not a church or denomination. We are a coalition of Christians from all sorts of backgrounds working together in pursuit of a common goal: gospel witness. Practically speaking, this means no formal rules and regulations govern our people as a whole. Some do stand closer to the center of the movement than do others. But the movement's center has shifted a bit as the movement has grown and adapted to change. It is impossible to get kicked out of the coalition altogether. Participation is voluntary. Adherents are largely self-selected. Plenty within our ranks (not least Roman Catholic and Orthodox Christians) choose to participate in the movement without affirming everything in it.

Second, evangelicals are descendants of the *Protestant* Reformation with a commitment to the *orthodoxy* (i.e., right doctrine and right worship) expressed in the ancient Christian creeds and promoted further by Reformers such as Luther, Zwingli, and Calvin—especially with regard to the gospel message. Some people disparage commitments to orthodoxy as repressive and narrow-minded, but evangelicals rarely do. Most of us will admit that the maintenance of orthodoxy can (and does at times) devolve into nasty witch hunts and power plays, but most of us also believe that this is in no way necessary—and that the alternative almost always proves much worse.[11]

Not all evangelicals are Protestants, and those who are belong to hundreds of Protestant denominations. Clearly, therefore, we do not all adhere to Protestant principles in precisely the same way. At the center of the movement, however, lies a firm commitment to the good news (*euangelion*) that "a man is justified by faith apart from observing the law" (Rom. 3:28). Most interpret this passage of Scripture in light of the Reformation doctrine that we are saved by grace alone (*sola gratia*) through faith alone (*sola fide*) in Christ alone (*solus Christus*). All agree that right doctrine comes from the canon of Scripture alone (*sola Scriptura*). In sum, evangelicals cling to the gospel message as spelled out in the Bible and seek to spread it as far and wide as limited resources allow.

Finally, modern evangelicals differ from other Christian groups in that the movement emerged from a definite, *eighteenth-century* cultural context, one that yielded a *twist* on Protestant orthodoxy. Modern evangelicals, as distinguished from others who use the label or share our view of the gospel message, are heirs of the Great Awakening—a renewal movement that changed forever the course of history. Chapter 2 discusses the history of that eighteenth-century awakening, highlighting the people, places, and events from which the movement took its rise.

Suggestions for Further Reading

Balmer, Randall. *Blessed Assurance: A History of Evangelicalism in America.* Boston: Beacon Press, 1999. A brief and breezy introduction to America's evangelicals aimed primarily at journalists and others interested in social and political issues. A good read from the most winsome writer on the subject.

———. *Mine Eyes Have Seen the Glory: A Journey into the Evangelical Subculture in America.* New York: Oxford University Press, 1989. A lively and personal glimpse at some of the most colorful patches on the quilt of what Balmer calls "America's folk religion."

Bebbington, David W. *Evangelicalism in Modern Britain: A History from the 1730s to the 1980s.* London: Unwin Hyman, 1989. The best scholarly survey of the history of evangelicalism in England, Scotland, and Wales.

Christian Scholar's Review 23 (September 1993). A special issue on the question, What is evangelicalism? The best place to go for Donald Dayton's take on America's evangelicals, as he unpacks it in opposition to what he calls the regnant "Presbyterian paradigm" (of George Marsden et al.).

Dayton, Donald W., and Robert K. Johnston, eds. *The Variety of American Evangelicalism*. Knoxville: University of Tennessee Press, 1991. The single best source on the diversity of America's evangelicals, Johnston's emphasis on our "family resemblance," and Dayton's "moratorium" on the evangelical label.

Hart, D. G. *Deconstructing Evangelicalism: Conservative Protestantism in the Age of Billy Graham*. Grand Rapids: Baker Academic, 2004. The best place to go for Hart's argument that evangelicalism does not exist and that churches would be better off if we stopped pretending that it did. "Without evangelicalism," Hart concludes, "Protestant Christianity may not be as unified . . . , but it will go on. And without the burden of forming a nationally influential coalition, American Protestants in all their Heinz 57 varieties . . . may even be healthier" (191).

Lippy, Charles H., and Robert H. Krapohl. *The Evangelicals: A Historical, Thematic, and Biographical Guide*. Westport, CN: Greenwood, 1999. The most helpful single-volume reference book on America's evangelicals. Includes a brief narrative history of the movement, scores of biographical articles on evangelical leaders, a time line, and other helps.

Marsden, George M. *Understanding Fundamentalism and Evangelicalism*. Grand Rapids: Eerdmans, 1991. The most accessible introduction to Marsden's take on evangelicalism. Largely a distillation and synthesis of his more specialized, scholarly writings.

McGrath, Alister. *Evangelicalism and the Future of Christianity*. Downers Grove, IL: InterVarsity, 1995. An engaging and optimistic (some have said triumphalistic) assessment of evangelicalism and its crucial role in the future of global Christianity.

Noll, Mark A. *American Evangelical Christianity: An Introduction*. Oxford: Blackwell, 2001. The best scholarly survey of American evangelical history. Especially strong on evangelical contributions to American politics, science, and culture.

2

A Surprising Work of God

The Eighteenth-Century Revival

Jesus declared, "I tell you the truth, no one can see the kingdom of God unless he is born again."

John 3:3

Modern evangelicalism emerged three centuries ago out of a spiritual movement the likes of which the world had never seen. Known then and since as the Great Awakening of Protestant Europe's state churches, this movement began in the middle of Europe, quickly spread to the British Isles and Britain's North American colonies, and soon impressed the entire West with the spiritual power of the new birth.

Before the Great Awakening, the Protestant world had been divided in both its worship and its witness by various ethnic and cultural boundaries. The heirs of the Reformation (which began in the 1510s) had long been fighting among themselves over matters of biblical interpretation and control of their churches' resources. Of course, the Protestant churches also yielded a vast spiritual harvest, blessing their members with biblical knowledge, a brand-new sense of gospel freedom, and the tools with which to practice their faith in lives of personal service. But in this chapter on the Awakening, I want to emphasize the limitations of early Protestantism so as to highlight the significance of the eighteenth-century twist.

During the Reformation itself, Catholics and Protestants had coexisted—though only just barely—by the power of the sword. They did often kill one another over religious (and other) differences. More often they lived and let live with the help of strong political leaders who protected their favorite forms of faith within their realms. In Germany, for example, the Peace of Augsburg (1555) temporarily placed a stay on Christian warfare with a principle later described as *cuius regio, eius religio* (whoever the king, his religion). In other parts of Europe, the Protestant movement established a foothold when and where sympathetic princes gave it sanctuary.

In the wake of the Reformation, Protestant leaders began *infighting* in much the same way as they fought the Catholics. Now dividing from one another over both piety and politics, they developed regional churches that fractured Christ's body further. This pattern of schism was symbolized vividly by the horrific Thirty Years' War (1618–48), during which tens of thousands of Christians lost their lives in the name of religion (among other causes). It culminated more peacefully in a new map of greater Europe featuring several variations on the traditional state-church theme. The Protestant princes who lived in most of Europe's German-speaking lands, as well as in parts of Scandinavia and even a few of the Slavic regions, adhered to the faith and practice of the Lutheran churches. Their peers who ruled in Switzerland, parts of southern and western Germany, northern Holland, parts of Hungary, and even much of Transylvania were Reformed, or Zwinglian/Calvinist, rather than Lutheran.[1] In Great Britain, Protestant rulers finally favored the Reformed but disagreed among themselves about how to practice their newfound faith. England's monarchs sponsored what many saw as a quasi-Catholic settlement, supervising what came to be called a uniquely "Anglican" Christianity. But many Scots struggled to win the right to practice Presbyterianism, a more strictly Calvinistic form of faith.

As a result of all this infighting, the Protestant world was broken apart, and its state churches were not the only signs of division. Its theologians developed competing Protestant confessions, or doctrinal statements, that buttressed their rulers' tendencies toward intramural partisanship. They fought theological battles with their fellow Protestant leaders. They encouraged the laity to think of themselves primarily as Calvinists or Arminians, as Lutherans or Anabaptists, rather than those who shared, in the words of St. Paul, "one Lord, one faith, one baptism" (Eph. 4:5). Consequently, they became ingrown. They rarely cooperated in missions. (As we will see later, some opposed cross-cultural missions altogether—on ostensibly biblical grounds.) They failed to offer a common witness to the world.

But during and after the Great Awakening, much of this changed for good—not overnight, and never completely, but considerably and noticeably. In a work of amazing grace and by the power of the Holy Spirit, untold numbers of Protestant leaders began to join hands across these boundaries and to collaborate in the work of gospel ministry. They did not establish a new church. Rather, they labored ecumenically—*inter*denominationally and *pan*-geographically—cosponsoring revivals, concerts of prayer, and common fasts. They traded pulpits with one another and promoted itinerant gospel preaching, thereby undermining the zoning system that had long divided their churches.

They accomplished these things with the help of a new communications network that linked evangelicals living in Europe and North America. Historians refer to the eighteenth century as the great age of letter writing. In God's providence, evangelicals could now stay in touch with one another quite easily, and they did, exchanging tens of thousands of pieces of correspondence. This was also the time of the rise of British magazines and newspapers, media used by Christians both to promote the cause of revival and to inform interested parties about God's work around the world. In fact, several Protestant leaders founded their own periodicals to convey intelligence regarding the progress of the gospel. Famous examples include George Whitefield's *Evangelical Magazine,* Thomas Prince's *Christian History,* James Robe's *Christian Monthly History,* and John Wesley's *Arminian Magazine.*

In every case, these publications provided their readers a sense of identity—a *new* sense of *religious* identity—that transcended their own national and denominational ties. Many now felt that they were a part of a new *international* movement of God. Their horizons expanded dramatically. Most importantly, they grew excited about reaching out in the name of Jesus rather than propping up much older and more parochial Protestant projects.

In short, the Great Awakening engendered a new sense of gospel urgency and a new spirit of cooperation. Of course, its evangelical leaders would never experience perfect peace, and the new movement they founded would know its fair share of sibling rivalry. But during and after these revivals, a host of new Protestant leaders submitted themselves "to be more vile" (in the famous words of John Wesley), to get off their high-church horses and to take the gospel to the streets—both at home and around the world. They preached in the fields, transgressed parish boundaries, and said that *the world* was now their parish, doing all they could to promote the cause of Christ. What's more, many made new friends with Protestant leaders in other places. They learned to trust one another's judgments. They came to see that their numerous differences need not keep them from working together.

This Great Awakening did have roots in several earlier Protestant movements that, while more limited in scope, paved the way for the revival. Before moving on to talk at length about the Awakening itself, therefore, this chapter says a word or two about the best-known of these earlier movements, British Puritanism and Continental Pietism.

British Puritanism

The Puritan movement emerged in England from dissatisfaction felt by many regarding the high-church Protestant settlement of Queen Elizabeth (1558–1603)[2] and her court. Numerous clergymen and their followers complained that their worship was still too Catholic—it was prescribed by laws, we must recall, that were enforced by the English Crown—and they called for further reformation of their nation's state church. The term *Puritan* was coined originally by those who made fun of these reformers and their purportedly prudish, self-righteous disposition. Eventually, however, it came to be used as a party label, referring to an assortment of Protestant activists who sought to *purify* the Church of England from within.

Generally speaking, the English Puritans lobbied for three main types of reform. First, they argued that pastors should root their preaching in God's Word—not perfunctorily but profoundly. They taught that a sermon is not an occasion for the display of human learning, nor should preachers major in moral platitudes or seek to shore up the status quo. Rather, preaching is serious business. As such, it should last for a very long time (Puritan sermons usually lasted for more than an hour), and it should "open" in simple terms the spiritual contents of the Bible. Second, the Puritans insisted that Sunday should be observed as the Christian Sabbath. It is a day of worship and rest, a day on which work and worldly amusements should be avoided at all costs. Third, the Puritans promoted what they called experimental religion or experiential Christianity, arguing that authentic, saving faith is first and foremost an affair of the heart. It cannot be inherited from one's parents or imposed on people from above. It requires an inward transformation, a real relationship with Christ.

The Puritans also opposed the retention of several Roman Catholic elements in the worship of their churches, demanding direct biblical warrant for all that was done on Sunday morning. Many refused to use the sign of the cross in the rite of Christian baptism. Some opposed the wearing of vestments (or special, liturgical clothes) by Anglican priests. Most opposed the practice of kneeling for the reception of the Lord's Supper. Some did not like organs or Christian images in the churches. In fact, the Puritans are notorious for destroying Christian art—not just crucifixes and stained-glass windows but even organs and their cases. Many adopted a stringent rule known as the "regulative principle," which stated that things not found in the Bible should not be found in worship either. Their agenda for the Church of England rested squarely on this rule. Indeed, their platform may be summarized as an attempt to strip away all that could conceivably get in the way of a sinner's reception and understanding of the Word. Convinced that God's Word and Spirit, not the externals of religion, save us, the Puritans sought above all else to help their neighbors meet God in person.

In the early years of their movement, the Puritans enjoyed a great deal of support among the gentry, in Parliament, and even from some in Elizabeth's court. But the queen herself resisted their push for radical reform, and when she died in 1603, she was succeeded to the throne by one who proved hostile to their cause.

King James I (1603–25), of the house of Stuart, was reared by Calvinists in Scotland, and, at first, Puritan leaders held out high hopes for him and his reign. Not wasting any time, they met him on his way to London with a "Millenary Petition" (so-called because it represented the wishes of one thousand clergymen), entreating the king to promote their cause from the royal throne. James decided to hold a conference at which their grievances would be heard, but when they asked for an end to episcopacy (the rule of the church by bishops), the king grew nervous and shut them down. "No bishop, no king," he declared, by which he meant that a less hierarchical governance of England's national church would surely undermine his own authority too. He threw them a bone by agreeing to sponsor a new translation of the Bible, known ever since as the King James Bible and completed seven years later (in 1611). But from then on he usually ignored or tried to suppress their calls for change.

James's son, King Charles I (1625–49), proved even more hostile to the Puritans. He married a French Catholic woman (Henrietta Maria), ruled without Parliament for more than a decade, and in 1633 appointed an ardent anti-Puritan, William Laud (1573–1645), archbishop of Canterbury. Together, Charles and Laud imposed an extremely high-church system on the entire English nation, fining and even jailing those who resisted. Many fearful Puritan sympathizers conformed to save their hides. Many others split from the church, often fleeing the country as well (the Pilgrim founders of Plymouth Colony were part of this separatist group). But tens of thousands stuck it out, doing their best to improve their church. Of these, some left for New England, where they could live more freely as Puritans (these were the founders of the largely nonseparatist Massachusetts Bay Colony). But most remained at home, where tensions mounted in church and state.

By 1642, an all-out rebellion began in Britain. Puritans gained control of Parliament, formed a rebel army—the New Model

Army, which was unusually well trained and highly effective—and soon ruled most of Britain uncontested. In 1645, they managed to execute William Laud. In 1649, they put to death the king himself. And from 1649 until the end of the 1650s, they ran the English government virtually by themselves. Oliver Cromwell (1599–1658), a member of Parliament as well as the captain of their army, proved the most powerful Puritan leader. In 1653, he dissolved the Parliament in London and became the sole "Lord Protector" of the nation.

After his death, however, the Puritan Interregnum (period "between the kingdom[s]") came to an end. Cromwell's son Richard (1626–1712) succeeded his father but proved unable to hold things together. As a result, the English gentry asked Charles II (1660–85) to take the throne. The son of Charles I, Charles II had been in hiding, and when he returned to public life, he cracked down hard on Puritanism. During the next two decades, in fact, he passed a series of laws in Britain that, practically speaking, outlawed the Puritans and their reforms once and for all. Roughly two thousand of them resisted and were deprived of their clerical offices. On his deathbed, Charles II made a profession of Catholic faith. In 1685, he was succeeded by his brother, James II (1685–88), who was by then already an open and ardent Catholic.

By this time the English people could no longer tolerate Catholic kings and thus invited the Protestant William of Orange (1688–1703) to take the British throne. Nevertheless, the Puritan movement had seen its demise. Some of the Puritans' leading concerns were shared by later dissenting ministers (i.e., those who dissented and separated themselves from England's established church) and wound up fueling the Great Awakening in Great Britain fifty years later. But Puritanism itself had failed to transform the Church of England, let alone exert great influence outside the British Empire.

Continental Pietism

By the second half of the seventeenth century, and like the Puritans in England, a group of Pietists began to call for church renewal in central Europe. Distressed by the dead orthodoxy they found in their state churches and in response to the dev-astation wrought by Europe's Thirty Years' War, they called for warmhearted Christian *piety*, emphasized practical Christian living, and worked to promote the kind of faith that made a real difference in everyday life.

At the academic level, they did this by pointing to Martin Luther's (1483–1546) own concern not only for doctrine but for the reformation of Christian practice as well. Most early Pietists were German, and, in their heavily Lutheran regions, this kind of appeal to the founding father of Protestantism was strategic. At the institutional level, they pursued their agenda on several fronts, most importantly by promoting small-group meetings for Bible study, common prayer, and accountability. Known as *collegia pietatis* (colleges of piety) or *ecclesiolae in ecclesia* (little churches within the church), these groups functioned much like present-day Christian cell groups. They provided their members a regular context for the personal expression of faith, encourag-ing everyone to appropriate their country's formal commitment to Christianity.

Though he built on the work of others—such as the Lutheran pastor, theologian, and spiritual writer Johann Arndt (1555–1621)—the "founding father" of the Pietist movement was a man named Philipp Jakob Spener (1635–1705), a German Lutheran who studied in Strasbourg and then served churches there and in Frankfurt. While in Frankfurt, Spener founded the Pietists' first college of piety in his home, to which he invited his parishioners twice a week. Before long the idea took off, and small-group meetings cropped up elsewhere, making Spener a household name in the Frankfurt area. In 1675, while still in Frankfurt serving his church, Spener published a book that became a clas-sic of Christian spirituality. Titled *Pia Desideria* (Holy Desires or Pious Desires), this volume also served as the charter of the fledgling Pietist movement.

Spener offered in this book what he called six "simple pro-posals" to the Christians of his day, hoping that God would use them to stir up the German churches. First, he proposed that Christians engage in personal Bible study, using Scripture to enhance their walk with God. Second, he proposed that laity perform priestly ministries, serving one another in love and embodying Luther's famous doctrine of the priesthood of all believers. Third, he proposed an emphasis on the practice of Christian faith, contending that Christianity was more than just a set of well-honed doctrines. Fourth, he proposed the charitable handling of all theological conflict, which he said should be pursued for the sake of changing people's hearts, not just scoring doctrinal points. Fifth, he proposed a restructuring of academic theological study, calling for higher standards of piety for students and their teachers. Sixth, he proposed the reform of Protestant preaching in his day, suggesting that sermons should serve primarily to edify those who hear them.

Though it called for little that Luther himself would not have approved, *Pia Desideria* became a controversial book (for its critique of the Christian establishment), and Spener soon became a rather controversial figure. The book made him enemies in Frankfurt as well as among the clergy at large. Therefore, in 1686, he decided to move to the province of Saxony, where he would serve as court preacher in the city of Dresden. He soon made enemies there as well—especially at Saxony's University of Leipzig, some of whose theological faculty strongly opposed the Pietists' goals—and moved to Berlin just five years later to serve as a parish pastor again. While there, he helped to found the new University of Halle (1694), which after his death became a nursery of German Pietism.

The second most famous early leader of the Pietists in Europe was a Lutheran scholar named August Hermann Francke (1663–1727). After studying philosophy and theology in both Erfurt and Kiel (Germany), Francke lectured at the University of Leipzig (1685). While there, he established controversial ties with Philipp Spener and began to promote the latter's proposals at the school. He held small-group Bible classes—sponsoring an academic version of the *collegia pietatis*—at which he advocated study more for devotional than scholarly reasons. Revival ensued and spread eventually throughout the city of Leipzig. But even as Francke's reputation grew as a scholar and a Pietist, he was dismissed from his post at Leipzig and asked to serve as a founding professor at the new University of Halle. He spent the rest of his ministry there, preparing pastors, training scholars, and founding an orphanage, a school for the poor (which met in his own home), a Christian publishing house, and a dispensary.

The Pietist movement itself did not survive the eighteenth century (at least not in a well-organized and integrated way), but Pietist practices and ideals continue to shape all kinds of churches—especially evangelical ones. *Collegia pietatis* continue to thrive around the globe. The Pietists set the standard for publishing Bibles for the laity (through their publishing house in Halle they printed more vernacular Bibles than any other group before them). They launched the first large-scale missions to other countries in Protestant history (approximately sixty Pietist missionaries were sent out from their school in Halle). Their parachurch work for the needy continues to inspire ministry leaders.

Like Spener, Francke became a lightning rod for the Pietists' many critics. But he also gained a large following and played a major role not only in renewing the German Lutheran churches but also in spreading the Pietist movement to other pockets of Europe—most notably Denmark and the Netherlands, whose Further Reformation (*Nadere Reformatie*) looked to both Puritanism and Pietism for resources.

The Transatlantic Great Awakening

Francke also played a role in preparing Europe for the Awakening, which he did not live to see himself. When it broke out in central Europe, it did so in several places at once. But most of the time the revivals occurred in regions of relative Pietist strength. What's more, the most prominent leader of the Awakening in central Europe was a man who had studied as a boy with Francke in Halle.

Nikolaus Ludwig Count von Zinzendorf (1700–1760) was a wealthy Saxon nobleman most famous for founding a Christian commune on one of his vast estates. Born in Dresden, he studied in Halle and at the University of Wittenberg before traveling in Holland and France, returning home, and settling down. He worked for a while in civil service, but as a Pietist student of Francke, Zinzendorf had a heart for gospel ministry. Beginning in 1722, he invited a group of Moravian refugees to live and worship at a place he called *Herrnhut* (The Lord's Watch, named for its location on the watch hill, or *Hutberg*, of his estate). The

Moravians descended from Jan Hus (c. 1372–1415)—the Bohemian (or Czech) martyr who paved the way for the Reformation—and a moderate group of his Hussite followers who had settled in Moravia (just east of Bohemia) as the *Unitas Fratrum*, or the church of United Brethren. As a result of the Thirty Years' War, the United Brethren were scattered and weak, but under Zinzendorf's able guidance, they enjoyed a religious revival in Saxony. Soon their community became a refuge for other beleaguered Protestants—Moravians, German Lutherans, Reformed believers, and Anabaptists—a new model of international, ecumenical partnership. All who lived there had to submit to a single apostolic rule, which yielded a spirit of solidarity and unity in mission.

The mission-mindedness of the Moravians served to multiply their influence, and soon they were playing a role in the Awakening of Britain as well. In fact, John Wesley (1703–91), the Awakening's leading light in England, was converted under the ministry of the Moravians. The fifteenth child of Susannah and Rev. Samuel Wesley (their seventh child to survive to adulthood), John was born in his father's parsonage in Epworth. Barely rescued from a fire that razed the house when he was only five, Wesley always considered himself a "firebrand plucked out of the burning" (Amos 4:11), or one preserved miraculously for a special purpose. After studying at Oxford and taking both bachelor's and master's degrees, he assisted his father at the parish church in Wroot. In 1729, he returned to Oxford to serve as a tutor and soon became involved in a new religious society. Modeled on the *collegia pietatis* of the Pietists in Germany, this society had been started by Wesley's younger brother Charles (1707–88)—the great poet, hymn writer, and gospel preacher. By 1730, it included a core group of five regular members referred to frequently by detractors as the Holy Club, the Bible moths, and, later, as the Methodists, for their methodical and fastidious biblical piety. By 1740, though, it was clear that three of these so-called Methodists (the two Wesleys and their colleague, George Whitefield) *had* been "plucked" by God for a purpose and were now leading a massive movement that revolutionized their church.[3]

From late in 1735 through early 1737, the Wesley brothers engaged in a mission to the Anglo-American colony of Georgia.

Georgia's governor, James Oglethorpe (1696–1785), had invited them there to serve—John as an Anglican chaplain, and Charles as Oglethorpe's secretary.[4] Their mission proved a failure. John's desire to preach to the Indians was thwarted by the governor (who wanted him working with the English). He fell in love but failed to win the heart of his girlfriend, Sophy Hopkey. Both he and Charles experienced difficulty relating to the colonists, most of whom were rugged pioneers and many of whom were ex-convicts. (Georgia was founded as a buffer between Britain's colonies farther north and the sometimes violent Spanish explorers and native Indians to the south—and thus was populated originally by parolees from debtors' prisons.)

Despite these setbacks, the venture became a milestone in John Wesley's life, as it provided him personal contact with the Moravians. A contingent of Zinzendorf's followers journeyed with him across the Atlantic (they too intended to preach the gospel to the native Americans, forming a beachhead in the New World for later Moravian immigration). During terrible storms at sea that scared John Wesley nearly to death, the Moravians demonstrated an amazing composure and steadfast Christian faith. Wesley noted in his journal that an especially dreadful storm broke out on January 25, 1736, as the Moravians gathered together for public worship:

> In the midst of the psalm wherewith their service began, the sea broke over, split the mainsail in pieces, covered the ship, and poured in between the decks, as if the great deep had already swallowed us up. A terrible screaming began among the English. The Germans [Moravians] calmly sung on. I asked one of them afterwards, "Was you not afraid?" He answered, "I thank God, no." I asked, "But were not your women and children afraid?" He replied mildly, "No; our women and children are not afraid to die."[5]

Stunned by their confidence in God's providence, Wesley "went to their crying, trembling [English] neighbours, and pointed out to them the difference in the hour of trial, between him that feareth God, and him that feareth him not."[6] He studied German every day so that he could speak to these hearty Christians. After returning to England depressed about his failures as a missionary, he concluded that though he had gone to Georgia to convert the native peoples, he had discovered along the way—with the help of Moravian friends—that he was in need of conversion himself.

Back in England, Wesley sought contact with the Moravians in London (they were already there spreading revival and seeking support for their missions work) and developed a friendship with a young Moravian minister, Peter Böhler (1712–75). Wesley continued to struggle spiritually, and Böhler prodded him to decide if he was sure that God had renovated his soul. Böhler also persuaded Wesley to join a Moravian small group known as the Fetter Lane Society of London. Over time, and under such influence, both John and Charles grew deeply anxious about their spiritual condition, their contacts with the Moravians yielding acute religious crises. Charles's turmoil ended first, when on May 21, 1738, he underwent a dramatic conversion. Three days later, at a society meeting on Aldersgate Street in London—inspired, again, by local Moravians—John's heart was "strangely warmed," as he would phrase it in his journal, during a reading of Luther's preface to the book of Romans. "I felt I did trust in Christ," he wrote, "Christ alone for salvation: And an assurance was given me, that he had taken away my sins, even mine, and saved me from the law of sin and death."[7] John Wesley, too, now knew conversion and the assurance of his salvation. His Aldersgate experience would change the world.

The very next Sunday, Wesley preached on the biblical doctrine of justification by God's grace alone (*sola gratia*), through faith alone (*sola fide*), in Christ alone (*solus Christus*). Three weeks later he left for *Herrnhut*, where he met with Zinzendorf personally. He remained a sensitive soul who knew both spiritual highs and spiritual lows. But he and Charles would spend the rest of their lives as leaders of the Awakening, giving shape to the new evangelical movement in England. Charles became the greatest writer of hymns in all of history. Though he preached a great deal too, he is best known for composing approximately 7,000 sacred poems, over 5,500 of which were set to music (including such beloved songs as "Hark! the Herald Angels Sing" and "Love Divine, All Loves Excelling"). For his part, John became the founder of the worldwide Methodist movement and the most influential organizer in evangelical history. He preached for another five decades, delivering 42,000 sermons and traveling 8,000 miles per year on horseback (totaling a quarter of a million miles altogether!). On the eve of his death, he was shepherding 294 Methodist preachers in England serving 71,668 Methodist faithful—not to mention the 43,265 Methodists in America.

Elsewhere in Britain, other leaders began to build on the momentum established for the Awakening, and soon most of the English-speaking world became involved. In Wales, Howell Harris (1714–73) became the leading revival preacher. Converted at a communion service in 1735—led by a man named Griffith Jones (1683–1761), the "morning star" of the Welsh revival—Harris went on to establish Calvinistic Methodism in Wales. In Scotland, a group of ministers led by Ebenezer Erskine (1680–1754) had been preaching the gospel in the fields for quite some time. In 1742, however, such efforts led to a massive revival, most famously in Cambuslang—led by a pastor named William McCulloch (1691–1771)—but also in lesser-known places such as Kilsyth, whose kirk (or church) was led by James Robe (1688–1753).

The best-known preacher in all the world during the height of the Great Awakening, and the one who best represents the Awakening's international orientation, was George Whitefield (1714–70)—friend of the Wesleys, Howell Harris, as well as the Scots. Born a poor boy in Gloucester, Whitefield lost his father when only one year old and as a child assisted his mother in running their local inn and tavern (the Bell Inn). Sent to Pembroke College, Oxford, in the fall of 1732, he worked his way through school as a servitor (a waiter and errand boy for Oxford's wealthier students). He joined the Wesleys' Holy Club in 1733, experienced conversion during Lent in the winter of 1735, received ordination as an Anglican deacon in 1736, and followed the Wesley brothers to Georgia in 1738 (where he founded an orphanage). Returning to England later that year, he began to preach in the open air (in the tradition of Erskine, Harris, and others), demonstrating remarkable skill as an extemporaneous speaker. (It was said that Whitefield could make people swoon by simply pronouncing "Mesopotamia.") Thousands flocked to hear him preach the gospel message in this way. He was ridiculed in the press, both for his sensational preaching style and for his conspicuous crossed eyes (a lifelong thorn in the flesh).

George Whitefield.
Used by permission of the National Portrait Gallery, Smithsonian Institution.

Despite such troubles, however, Whitefield became the revival's most visible leader, traversing the globe to promote the new birth and connecting revival proponents everywhere by means of his global ministry.

It was Whitefield, in fact, who first persuaded John Wesley to take up field preaching (one of the hallmarks of the Awakening)—much as Wesley had earlier coaxed the younger Whitefield into Georgia. In March of 1739, Whitefield was ready to resume his preaching ministry in the colonies but was leading a major revival in the fields outside Bristol. Unwilling to leave the people of Bristol entirely bereft of gospel ministry, he wrote to Wesley asking for help. Wesley was floored, for though he believed in the need for evangelistic preaching, he was also a high-church Anglican who placed a high premium on propriety. As he confessed in his spiritual journal, "I could scarce reconcile myself at first to this strange way of preaching in the fields . . . having been all my life (till very lately) so tenacious of every point relating to decency and order, that I should have thought the saving of souls almost a sin, if it had not been done in a church."[8] Whitefield persisted, however, and on April 2, 1739, Wesley "submitted to be more vile, and proclaimed in the highways the glad tidings of salvation, speaking from a little eminence in a ground adjoining to the city [of Bristol], to about three thousand people."[9]

Whitefield's second trip to the colonies also proved a great success—so much so, in fact, that he made five subsequent trips to America, during the last of which he died and was buried in Massachusetts (admirers continue to view his crypt in Newburyport today). All in all, Whitefield preached over seventy-five hundred American sermons to crowds that frequently numbered in the tens of thousands. It is difficult to communicate to contemporary Christians—whose lives are cluttered with mass media and who are now used to extempore preaching—the awesome power of Whitefield's sermons in the lives of those who heard them first. But perhaps an account that survives from a farmer who was converted under this preaching—a Connecticut man named Nathan Cole (1711–83)—will convey the feelings that people associated with Whitefield, feelings that fueled the rise of evangelicalism.

> Now it pleased God to send Mr. Whitefield into this land and my hearing of his preaching at Philadelphia, like one of the old apostles, and many thousands flocking after him to hear the gospel and great numbers converted to Christ, I felt the Spirit of God drawing me by conviction. . . . One morning, all on a sudden, about 8 or 9 o'clock there came a messenger and said, "Mr. Whitefield preached at Hartford and Wethersfield yesterday and is to preach at Middletown this morning at 10 o'clock." I was in my field, at work, I dropped my tool that I had in my hand and ran home and ran through my house and bade my wife get ready quick to go and hear Mr. Whitefield preach at Middletown and ran to my pasture for my horse with all my might, fearing I should be too late to hear him. I brought my horse home and soon mounted and took my wife up and went forward as fast as

I thought the horse could bear, and when my horse began to be out of breath I would get down and put my wife in the saddle and bid her ride as fast as she could and not stop or slack for me except I bade her, and so I would run until I was almost out of breath and then mount my horse again, and so I did several times to favour my horse . . . for we had twelve miles to ride double in little more than an hour.

On high ground I saw before me a cloud or fog rising, I first thought off from the great river [the Connecticut River] but as I came nearer the road I heard a noise something like a low rumbling of horses feet coming down the road and this cloud was a cloud of dust made by the running of horses feet. It arose some rods in the air, over the tops of the hills and trees, and when I came within about twenty rods of the road I could see men and horses slipping along in the cloud like shadows and when I came nearer it was like a steady stream of horses and their riders, scarcely a horse more than his length behind another, all of a lather and some with sweat. . . .

We went down with the stream, I heard no man speak a word all the way, three miles, but everyone pressing forward in great haste, and when we got down to the old meetinghouse there was a great multitude—it was said to be 3 or 4000 people assembled together. We got off from our horses and shook off the dust, and the ministers were then coming to the meetinghouse. I turned and looked towards the great river and saw ferry boats running swift, forward and backward, bringing over loads of people, the oars rowed nimble and quick. Everything, men, horses and boats, all seemed to be struggling for life.[10]

Struggling for life, indeed. Many thousands of people dated their new life in Christ to such occasions. Tens of thousands joined the churches during the heyday of the Awakening. What's more, Whitefield proved to be the era's greatest media figure, selling more publications than anyone else in America at the time (1739–45), receiving advanced publicity and widespread coverage in the public press (most famously in Benjamin Franklin's *Pennsylvania Gazette*), and frequently drafting the copy himself! In short, by 1740, Whitefield was a worldwide gospel sensation. While secular scholars tend to focus on Whitefield's social significance, God used his fame to spread the good news. It is no coincidence that most evangelical pastors since his day have modeled their preaching after Whitefield's (whether consciously or not). In the words of Sarah Edwards (1710–58):

> It is wonderful to see what a spell he casts over an audience by proclaiming the simplest truths of the Bible. I have seen upwards of a thousand people hang on his words with breathless silence, broken only by an occasional half-suppressed sob. He impresses the ignorant, and not less the educated and refined. It is reported that while the miners of England listened to him, the tears made white furrows down their smutty cheeks. So here, our mechanics shut up their shops, and the day-labourers throw down their tools, to go and hear him preach, and few return unaffected. . . . He speaks from a heart all aglow with love, and pours out a torrent of eloquence which is almost irresistible.[11]

Whitefield was not alone in preaching revival in the colonies. In fact, he had many American colleagues working hard to promote the Awakening. Descendants of the Puritans, such as New England's Solomon Stoddard (1643–1729), had led revival "harvests" since the seventeenth century. In England's middle colonies, the German-born Pietist Theodore Frelinghuysen (1691–c. 1747) and Scots-Irish Presbyterians such as William (1673–1746) and Gilbert Tennent (1703–64), had been evangelizing the churches since the 1720s and 1730s (especially the Dutch Reformed and Presbyterian churches of New Jersey and Pennsylvania).[12] To the south, men such as the Presbyterian minister Samuel Davies (1723–61) and the Baptist Shubal Stearns (1706–71) led revivals beginning in the 1750s (primarily in Virginia and North Carolina).

But it was Sarah Edwards's husband, the Congregationalist Jonathan Edwards (1703–58), who proved the single most important evangelical in America. A friend of Whitefield and many leading evangelicals in Scotland, one whose works were reprinted in England (by John Wesley), Scotland, Wales, and on the Continent (at first in German and in Dutch), Edwards quickly became the theological genius of the Awakening.

The fifth child and only son of Esther Stoddard Edwards (daughter of Solomon Stoddard) and Rev. Timothy Edwards, Jonathan Edwards entered the world in his parents' parsonage in East Windsor, Connecticut. He began to study Latin at the tender age of six. Before he turned thirteen, he was reading Greek and

Jonathan Edwards.

Used by permission of the Stockbridge Library Association Historical Collection.

Hebrew as well. In September of 1716, he matriculated at Yale (he was only twelve years old). In the fall of 1720, he graduated first in his class. From 1720 to 1722, he studied at Yale for a master's degree, during which time he experienced conversion (in May or June of 1721) and prepared himself for pastoral ministry. As he recounted many years later in what is known as his "Personal Narrative," a remarkable document that has long shaped evangelical notions of the new birth, his conversion at Yale proved a truly life-changing, mind-altering experience:

> The first that I remember that ever I found anything of that sort of inward, sweet delight in God and divine things, that I have lived much in since, was on reading those words, 1 Tim. 1:17, "Now unto the King eternal, immortal, invisible, the only wise God, be honor and glory forever and ever, Amen." As I read the words, there came into my soul, and was as it were diffused through it, a sense of the glory of the divine being; a new sense, quite different from anything I ever experienced before. Never any words of Scripture seemed to me as these words did. I thought with

myself, how excellent a Being that was; and how happy I should be, if I might enjoy that God, and be wrapt up to God in heaven, and be as it were swallowed up in him. I kept saying, and as it were singing over these words of Scripture to myself; and went to prayer, to pray to God that I might enjoy him; and prayed in a manner quite different from what I used to do; with a new sort of affection. . . . From about that time, I began to have a new kind of apprehensions and ideas of Christ, and the work of redemption, and the glorious way of salvation by him. I had an inward, sweet sense of these things, that at times came into my heart; and my soul was led away in pleasant views and contemplations of them. And my mind was greatly engaged, to spend my time in reading and meditating on Christ; and the beauty and excellency of his person, and the lovely way of salvation, by free grace in him. . . . And [I] found, from time to time, an inward sweetness, that used . . . to carry me away in my contemplations; in what I know not how to express otherwise, than by a calm, sweet abstraction of soul from all the concerns o[f] this world. . . . The sense I had of divine things, would often of a sudden . . . kindle up a sweet burning in my heart; an ardor of my soul, that I know not how to express.[13]

Beginning in August of 1722, Edwards pastored his first congregation, an English Presbyterian church in New York, but by the following April he was working at home again, completing his master's thesis on justification by faith (delivered in Latin at Yale's commencement in September of 1723). Shortly after graduation, he began to preach in Bolton, Connecticut, and considered settling down there at the Congregational church. The following summer, though, he accepted a job as a teacher at Yale, where he remained for nearly two years and almost worked himself to death before he was called to serve as assistant pastor to his grandfather Solomon Stoddard. He moved to Northampton, Massachusetts, late in 1726. He received his ordination there the following February and married Sarah Pierpont (another preacher's kid) on July 28, 1727. On February 11, 1729, Stoddard passed away, leaving the twenty-five-year-old Edwards the sole pastor of a church that boasted nearly seven hundred members.

Edwards soon led a revival there that anticipated the Awakening. In 1734, and while still in his early thirties, he began to

Sarah Pierpont Edwards.

Joseph Badger, *Mrs. Jonathan Edwards (Sarah Pierpont) (1710–1758)*. Bequest of Eugene Phelps Edwards. Used by permission of the Yale University Art Gallery.

preach a lengthy sermon series on justification by faith (based on his master's thesis at Yale), which was by now a major doctrine of the emergent evangelicals. Before he knew it, revival broke out, and hundreds of locals experienced conversion. The revival spread to other churches along the Connecticut River Valley, and Edwards wrote an account of this work at the behest of Christians in London titled *A Faithful Narrative of the Surprising Work of God* (1737). The book was published in London and Boston, then in Germany and Holland, inspiring excitement around the world regarding this work of the Holy Spirit. Edwards's story encouraged John Wesley in his decision to preach out of doors. It excited Whitefield about the promise of gospel preaching in the colonies. Only a few years later much of the (Western) world was aflame with the Spirit, the various regional revival efforts of the Puritans and the Pietists panning out in a wide-scale, international Awakening.

By early 1740, the Great Awakening hit its peak. This work of God that began in Europe had now spread all the way to America, and Christians all over the West believed that the Spirit was building the church in a manner unprecedented in scope (many believed, in fact, that the millennium was near). This was certainly not the first time the church had seen revival, but it was the first time that Protestants worked so well together, transcending their narrower, ethnic, regional, and denominational interests for the sake of cooperation in mission.

Edwards enabled this common witness as much as anyone else at the time by means of a series of books that helped to explain the revivals and their meaning. To Christians struggling to make sense of the signs and wonders they were witnessing, Edwards gave practical, biblical guidance in well-known treatises such as *Distinguishing Marks of a Work of the Spirit of God* (1741), *Some Thoughts Concerning Revival* (1742), and, most importantly, a major work called the *Religious Affections* (1746).

Just as significantly, to Calvinists harboring qualms about the Awakening and its use of "indiscriminate" evangelism—or the revivalists' practice of extending the gospel promises to *everyone* in their audiences, without stressing that God redeems only those elected for salvation—Edwards provided an analysis in the *Freedom of the Will* (1754) that distinguished clearly between a nonelect sinner's "natural ability" (or constitutional capacity) to repent and turn from sin and his or her "moral inability" (or ineradicable unwillingness) to do the same. It may seem strange today that religious conservatives opposed the Great Awakening, that there were Calvinists at the time whose views of election and predestination kept them from preaching the good news to people outside their own communities. But by the time of the Awakening, a long and hallowed tradition existed in Great Britain, especially, whose adherents thought it presumptuous to suggest to perfect strangers that it was possible for *any* of them to repent and be reborn. (In Edwards's day, English Baptists such as John Gill [1697–1771] and John Brine [1703–65] taught that this could be said with confidence only within the confines of a rightly ordered, covenanted community.) Edwards's theology cleared the way for many such people to back the Awakening and to evangelize outside their own churches and ethnic groups. It helped them preach the gospel freely without suggesting in the process that non-Christians had the power to save themselves.

As this story suggests, the Awakening did generate its fair share of religious controversy. The revivals divided families, congregations, and communities, and the Awakening as a whole realigned the Protestant world. Edwards's church ejected him in June of 1750 as the result of local troubles exacerbated by the revivals. Wesley and Whitefield parted ways during the early 1740s over what seemed for a short while to be insurmountable differences—Wesley was an Arminian, and Whitefield was a Calvinist—developing two separate Methodist traditions in Great Britain. The Moravians suffered through a period known as "the time of sifting" (1745–49), during which some within their ranks went off the deep end theologically.

But a movement had been born, one that would change the face of the world. Orthodox Protestants now collaborated on a global scale, forming a new and truly multicultural movement of the Spirit. Soon this movement grew more important to those engaged in gospel missions than the boundaries that had long shaped—and severely limited—their identities. As Whitefield declared to a friend in May of 1742, "If the Lord gives us a true catholic spirit, free from a party sectarian zeal, we shall do well . . . for I am persuaded, unless we all are content to preach Christ, and to keep off from disputable things, wherein we differ, God will not bless us long. If we act otherwise, however we may talk of a catholic spirit, we shall only be bringing people over to our own party, and there fetter them. I pray the Lord to keep . . . me from such a spirit."[14] In the 1740s, thousands of others began to pray in this way too.

Suggestions for Further Reading

Brown, Dale W. *Understanding Pietism*. Grand Rapids: Eerdmans, 1978. A good, simple introduction to the Pietist movement.

Dallimore, Arnold A. *George Whitefield: The Life and Times of the Great Evangelist of the Eighteenth-Century Revival.* 2 vols. Carlisle, PA: Banner of Truth Trust, 1970. An explicitly Christian biography of Whitefield written by an admirer. Based largely on Luke Tyerman's classic nineteenth-century *Life of George Whitefield.* Exhaustive in detail.

Hindmarsh, Bruce. *John Newton and the English Evangelical Tradition: Between the Conversions of Wesley and Wilberforce.* 1996; reprint, Grand Rapids: Eerdmans, 2000. A wonderful scholarly treatment of the author of "Amazing Grace" and his role in the emergent evangelical movement in England. Best on the British background of the evangelical movement and on Newton's crucial role as a "broker of consensus" within the movement "whose spirituality and manner of theological formulation represented an ideal of evangelical catholicity" (327).

Lambert, Frank. *Inventing the "Great Awakening."* Princeton: Princeton University Press, 1999. For now, the standard scholarly history of America's Great Awakening. Needlessly trendy in its assertion that the revival leaders themselves "invented" the scope and coherence of the Awakening but reliable and up-to-date in its presentation of information.

Marsden, George M. *Jonathan Edwards: A Life.* New Haven: Yale University Press, 2003. The definitive scholarly biography of Edwards.

Murray, Iain H. *Jonathan Edwards: A New Biography.* Carlisle, PA: Banner of Truth Trust, 1987. A great read from an expert Christian biographer and avid admirer of Edwards. At times Murray's Edwards (or the man Murray wanted Edwards to be) overshadows the real Edwards. But this book offers an edifying assessment of Edwards's life and ministry from an explicitly Christian point of view.

Noll, Mark A. *The Rise of Evangelicalism: The Age of Edwards, Whitefield, and the Wesleys.* A History of Evangelicalism: People, Movements, and Ideas in the English-Speaking World, vol. 1. Downers Grove, IL: InterVarsity, 2003. A masterful yet plain-style account of the rise of evangelicalism in its eighteenth-century, Anglo-American context. Part of a promising new series overseen by David Bebbington (a total of five volumes are scheduled for publication).

Podmore, Colin. *The Moravian Church in England, 1728–1760.* Oxford: Oxford University Press, 1998. The best treatment of the Moravians' contribution to the Awakening in England.

Rack, Henry D. *Reasonable Enthusiast: John Wesley and the Rise of Methodism.* 2nd ed. Nashville: Abingdon, 1993. The most sophisticated scholarly treatment of John Wesley's life and ministry.

Stoeffler, F. Ernest. *Continental Pietism and Early American Christianity.* Grand Rapids: Eerdmans, 1976. A somewhat dated but still helpful introduction to the Pietists' influence in America.

Stout, Harry S. *The Divine Dramatist: George Whitefield and the Rise of Modern Evangelicalism.* Grand Rapids: Eerdmans, 1991. A highly acclaimed and controversial interpretation of Whitefield's ministry. Written by a Christian but from a largely secular point of view. Its author teaches at Yale University as the Jonathan Edwards Professor of American Christianity.

Tracy, Joseph. *The Great Awakening: A History of the Revival of Religion in the Time of Edwards and Whitefield.* 1842; reprint, Carlisle, PA: Banner of Truth Trust, 1976. A classic Christian interpretation of the Awakening written by an evangelical pastor and promoter of revival.

Ward, W. R. *The Protestant Evangelical Awakening.* Cambridge: Cambridge University Press, 1992. The definitive scholarly survey of the entire transatlantic Awakening. Especially strong on the Continental European origins of the revivals. Somewhat difficult for nonspecialists to read and understand.

Wood, Arthur Skevington. *The Burning Heart: John Wesley, Evangelist.* Grand Rapids: Eerdmans, 1967. A warmhearted treatment of Wesley's ministry by a Methodist pastor and evangelist. Inspiring reading for evangelicals.

3

Crafting New Wineskins

Institutionalizing the Movement

"But what about you?" he [Jesus] asked. "Who do you say I am?"

Simon Peter answered, "You are the Christ, the Son of the living God."

Jesus replied, "Blessed are you, Simon son of Jonah, for this was not revealed to you by man, but by my Father in heaven. And I tell you that you are Peter, and on this rock I will build my church, and the gates of Hades will not overcome it. I will give you the keys of the kingdom of heaven; whatever you bind on earth will be bound in heaven, and whatever you loose on earth will be loosed in heaven."

Matthew 16:15–19

Those charged with maintaining the church's ministries usually require institutions in which to carry on their work. But for the most part, evangelicals have chafed at this fact of life. It is nearly impossible to perpetuate even the loftiest spiritual movements without some planning, organization, and corporate support.

53

But budgets, bricks, and mortar so often squelch the work of the Spirit that evangelicals tend to avoid—and even oppose—the steady grind of bureaucracy. To be sure, we have harbored our fair share of empire-building entrepreneurs, but we have not been good "company men." We have erred most often, in fact, by failing to take our social structures seriously. As people committed to surmounting social boundaries with the gospel, we often neglect the institutions needed to further kingdom work.

Evangelicals are not alone in neglecting institutions. As numerous writers have noted, church history abounds with a chronic tension between Spirit and structure, or dynamic spirituality and its static, albeit necessary, structural supports. Some point to a pattern in Christian history in which no sooner are the church and its institutions revitalized than the agents of change seek to conserve their renewal in (new) institutional forms. These forms themselves become petrified, and those dependent on the forms languish in need of revival again. Such history has hardly inspired confidence in the promise of institutions.

But though evangelicals do not suffer by themselves from this chronic tension, the history of evangelicalism epitomizes for many the deep frustration that it yields—passionate as evangelicals are in pursuit of a vibrant spirituality—as well as the turbulent social life so often associated with it. Ever since the Great Awakening, we have imagined ourselves on a cycle of revival and decline, making the greatest spiritual strides in major seasons of renewal. In attempting to regularize revival, to bottle our leaders' moral charisma, to coordinate the projects needed to shore up the life of the Spirit, we have built new structures that can preserve, channel, and multiply our energies. Over and over again, however, these structures themselves have become corrupt, disenchanting the movement's purists and leading to further reformation.

Ironically, this cycle of revival and decline has created countless evangelical institutions, each one needed to resurrect the life of its predecessors. These institutions, furthermore, have contributed to the development of a schismatic party spirit, the very thing that Whitefield prayed against at the height of the Great Awakening. They have severed families, congregations, even entire denominations, restructuring the spiritual landscape of our country—and the world. They have also sponsored the rise of a massive evangelical subculture, a spiritual counterculture of sorts but one now nearly self-sufficient from an institutional point of view and frequently isolated from the groups it emerged in the first place to renew.

This chapter begins to explain how this state of affairs has come to be by charting the early institutional work of the evangelical movement, stressing the tension we have felt in trying to structure the life of the Spirit. As much as any other group in the long history of Christianity, evangelicals have been wary of the dangers of institutions (regular practices, relationships, and organizational structures that shape and limit our ministries). But like every other movement concerned to make a social difference, evangelicalism has discovered that institutions are essential.

Revival Era Realignments

No sooner did the Great Awakening hit America's shores than it led to some major realignments in its people's religious lives. In the colonies of New York, Pennsylvania, and New Jersey, it split the Presbyterian Church into rival "New Side" and "Old Side" synods, the former led by Gilbert Tennent, pushing revival and renewal and largely responsible for the founding of the College of New Jersey in 1746 (later Princeton University). In the South, it revolutionized the liturgical, hierarchical, heavily Anglican way of life as evangelical insurgents battled against what they considered social and spiritual oppression (the Anglican Church was established by law in the South, and its leaders usually resisted evangelical encroachments). As we will see in chapter 4, it yielded a harvest of Indian Christians. Hundreds of Native Americans joined the ranks of those who were born again, and a surge of Indian missions paved the way for political partnerships that bolstered the English against the French and their own aboriginal allies. As we will learn in chapter 5, the Awakening also made deep inroads among America's African slaves, contributing powerfully to the formation of the historic black churches.

But nowhere did the Awakening produce more spiritual institutions than in New England, the regional center of early

American evangelicalism. For several decades after the rise of the transatlantic Great Awakening, New England led the way in constructing new evangelical organizations, often dividing and even destroying older structures in the process. Beginning as early as 1740, this region's "standing order" churches, the Congregationalists—state-supported scions of the Puritans—fractured into several "New" and "Old Light" factions. The Old Light faction fought most forcefully over the "enthusiasm" attending the revival and the itinerant preaching ministries of its New Light organizers. The struggle eventually sundered more than one hundred congregations and led to a movement of "separates" who planted new, sectarian worship centers.[1]

In our own, more placid age of evangelical ascendance, we often forget the contentiousness of early evangelical leaders. But at the height of the Awakening, many enlisted in what they viewed as eternally sanctioned spiritual warfare, struggling valiantly over the destinies of countless thousands of souls. In 1740, for example, Whitefield exclaimed at Harvard and Yale that the scholars' "light had become darkness" and needed kindling once again. In April of 1741, Gilbert Tennent preached over seventeen times within the span of a week to the patient people of New Haven, warning Yale's "modern Pharisees" not to hide their dead hearts behind a veneer of scholarship. Three months later, James Davenport (1716–57) denounced New Haven's minister from the pulpit of his own church—while he was sitting in the audience! He dubbed Rev. Joseph Noyes (1688–1761) a vicious "wolf in sheep's clothing" and urged parishioners to separate from his ministry. Later that fall, David Brainerd (1718–47), who went on to pioneer missions to the Indians of New Jersey, was expelled from Yale for insulting one of his teachers, Chauncey Whittelsy (1717–87). "He has no more grace than a chair," the adolescent Brainerd charged. By the following spring, many others at Yale grew spiritually disrespectful, and the rector, Thomas Clap (1703–67), closed the school and sent the boys home.[2] Before long, the general assembly of Connecticut raised concern and passed a law against unlicensed itinerancy.

No wonder, then, that by the time New England's revivals subsided at least four major parties were competing for adherents. The most controversial of the four was known as the radical New Lights. They became separatists at the apex of the Awakening, denouncing the Congregational ministry as apostate. Not all of them proved as pugnacious as the notorious James Davenport. Most, in fact, were truly concerned about the spiritual health of the region. Unfortunately, however, Davenport's inflammatory antics have symbolized for most the divisiveness they often provoked. One incident, especially, caught the attention of their critics. As reported at length (and rather sarcastically) in the *Boston Weekly Post-Boy*, Davenport preached in New London, Connecticut, in March of 1743, "accompanied with Three Armour-Bearers [!], and some others."

> Upon his Arrival, the Christians . . . gather'd round about him in Crouds, who paid him such profound Respect, Reverence and Homage, that his well-known great Modesty and Humility oblig'd him to check their Devotion, by telling them, he was not a God, but a Man. . . . On the 6th [of March], it being the Lord's Day, just before the Conclusion of the Publick Worship, and also as the People were returning from the House of God, they were surpriz'd with a great Noise and Out-cry; Multitudes hasten'd toward . . . one of the most public Places in the Town, and there found these good People encompassing a Fire which they had built up in the Street, into which they were casting Numbers of Books, principally on Divinity, and those that were well-approved by Protestant Divines. . . . Nothing can be more astonishing than their insolent Behaviour was during the Time of their Sacrifice, as 'tis said they call'd it; whilst the Books were in the Flames they cry'd out, "Thus the Souls of the Authors of those Books, those of them that are dead, are roasting in the Flames of Hell"; and that "the Fate of those surviving, would be the same, unless speedy Repentance prevented."
>
> On the next Day they had at the same Place a second Bonfire of the like Materials, and manag'd in the same manner. Having given this fatal Stroke to "Heresy," they made ready to attack "Idolatry." . . . Mr. Davenport told them . . . that they themselves were guilty of idolizing their Apparel, and should therefore divest themselves of those Things especially which were for Ornament, and let them be burnt: Some of them in the height of their Zeal, conferred not with Flesh and Blood, but fell to stripping and cast their Cloaths down at their Apostle's Feet; one or two hesitated about the Matter, and were so bold as to tell him they had nothing on which they idoliz'd: He reply'd, that such and such a Thing was an Offence to him; and they must down with them. . . . Mr. Davenport pray'd

himself; and . . . took his wearing Breeches [i.e., his trousers], and hove them with Violence into the Pile, saying, "Go you with the Rest." A young Sister, whose Modesty could not bear to see the Mixture of Cloaks, Petty Coats and Breeches, snatch'd up his Breeches, and sent them at him, with . . . much Indignation. . . . At this Juncture came in a Brother from a neighbouring Town; a Man of more Sense than most of them have; and apply'd warmly to Mr. Davenport, told him, He was "making a Calf," and that he thot', "the Devil was in him." Mr. Davenport said, He "tho't so too"; and added, That he "was under the Influence of an evil Spirit, and that God had left Him."[3]

Many observers, including Davenport, now questioned his mental health. The following year, he published a series of *Confessions and Retractions*. His peers ultimately restored him to the Presbyterian ministry, and he went on to serve several New Side congregations in New Jersey. But by then he and others of the separatist persuasion had given opponents of revival a host of reasons to throw the baby out with the bath water.

These opponents comprised the second of the four major parties competing for souls at the close of the Awakening. They called themselves the Old Lights. Led by the venerable Charles Chauncy (1705–87), pastor of Boston's First Church, they presented themselves as defenders of the religious status quo. The social network that held them together eventually bred religious liberalism, as Chauncy and his circle first adopted universalism (the doctrine that everyone will eventually be saved), and their descendants at Harvard went on to champion Unitarianism (an anti-Calvinist movement known for denying the doctrine of the Trinity). But during the Awakening itself, these men restricted themselves to condemning evangelical "enthusiasm" and promoting a rational and temperate Christian piety.

A third group emerged a decade after the Awakening to resist the growing influence of Jonathan Edwards and his disciples. Led by the likes of Moses Mather (1719–1806) and Yale president Ezra Stiles (1727–95), they called themselves "Old Calvinists" and criticized the novelty of the "New Divinity," the theological movement based on Edwards's ministry. These Old Calvinists died out during the Second Great Awakening (discussed below). They never enjoyed the numbers or the power of the other three groups, but for roughly half a century they contributed to the cacophony of voices disagreeing over the future of New England.

The Edwardsians, however, the fourth group of Congregationalists, would win the fervent struggle for New England's hearts and minds. Led by Edwards and associates such as Joseph Bellamy (1719–90), Samuel Hopkins (1721–1803), and Timothy Dwight (1752–1817), they positioned themselves as moderate promoters of the revival (i.e., moderate New Lights), steering a course between the Old Lights and the excesses of the radicals.

The New Divinity of the Edwardsians dealt primarily with the experience of revival and conversion. As Calvinists, they taught that none could come to faith in Christ except by supernatural grace, but as evangelists, they knew that saving grace came through the gospel. So they preached the glad tidings as far and wide as their voices would carry. They cried "whosoever will may come," and they claimed that sinners had what they called a *natural ability* to believe. They knew that only God's elect would be reborn and persevere, but they sought to rid the unrepentant of lame excuses for their sin. Everyone gets what he or she wants, the Edwardsian evangelists proclaimed. The problem is that rebellious sinners do not *want* to repent and submit to God. They have a constitutional capacity—a physical capability—to comply with the gospel offer, but their hearts are in the wrong place. They will not kneel at the foot of the cross.[4]

As noted in chapter 2, this dual commitment to natural ability and moral inability enabled many Calvinists to participate in revival—calling their hearers indiscriminately to immediate repentance (i.e., whether or not everyone listening was predestined for salvation). But it sounded strangely new and even dangerous to Old Calvinists, who claimed the high ground of tradition but had less success converting the lost.

The Edwardsian commitment to conversion also enabled Reformed pastors to push for renewal in their churches, purifying their congregations by driving home the important differences between true and false religion. As Edwards preached to his parishioners in the midst of the Awakening, "There is such a thing as conversion," and "'tis the most important thing in the world; and they are happy that have been the subjects of it and they most miserable that have not."[5] In a state-church setting like that in New England—where everyone had to attend church and support its ministries with their taxes—this theme was crucial to the spiritual health of the people. The Edwardsians resisted separatism; they stayed within the state churches. But in the tradition of the Puritans, they purified them from within, calling parishioners to regenerate (or born-again) Christian discipleship.

New Divinity theologians developed other distinctive doctrines, but they won their region's churches with their institutional work. They came to dominate New England's ministerial associations, playing a major role in examining and licensing future pastors. Ministering as they did before the rise of modern seminaries, they founded "schools of the prophets" (*schola prophetarum*) in which to train the future clergy. Seasoned pastors led the schools, welcoming recent college graduates headed for ministry into their homes, supervising their doctrinal study, and letting them practice preaching and counseling in their churches under their watch. They spread Edwardsian doctrinal views by publishing scores of tracts and treatises—both Edwards's and their own. They organized concerts of prayer, common fasts, and evangelistic conference meetings to pull New England together in support of the revivals. Finally, they worked at tightening their churches' sacramental practice, reversing a century-old tradition that allowed upstanding attenders unable to testify to conversion to participate in the Lord's Supper anyway. The net effect of these endeavors was that by the end of the eighteenth century the vast majority of New England's churches were Edwardsian; many separates, now satisfied with the fruit of Edwardsianism, pulled up stakes and rejoined the standing order; and Edwards's followers stood poised to lead another major revival, known ever since in the annals of history as the Second Great Awakening.

The eighteenth-century revivals did not turn out as Edwards had hoped. They caused division and spiritual rancor. Moreover, their evangelical leaders were now but one of several groups competing for people's religious allegiances. Ironically, however, while the Awakening split the very churches its leaders set out to renew, it also secured for them a niche from which to prosecute their agenda. By the end of the eighteenth century, they took advantage of this position to infiltrate the Western world with the spirit and structures of revival.

Disestablishment and the Rise of Evangelical Denominations

It is no coincidence that the rise of the modern evangelical movement took place at roughly the same time as the decline of Christendom.[6] Throughout most of Christian history, the gospel was spread more often than not by the territorial expansion of Christian nations—nations with legally "established" churches, the will to colonize foreign lands, and the audacity to Christianize their populations by force. In the eighteenth and nineteenth centuries, however, most state churches in the West began to weaken—along with their goal of imposing religious unity. Modern thinkers began to defend the right to freedom of religion, the official leaders of state churches lost much of their secular authority, and the kind of religious toleration that most Americans now expect began to find its champions in the halls of power.

Early on, most evangelicals were nervous about these trends. They feared the loss of Christian influence on America's cultural life. They also opposed the "infidelity" (unfaithfulness or unbelief) of the more open, liberal champions of religious toleration. Eventually, however, evangelicals embraced the social order these trends produced and exploited it to promote their *transdenominational* movement. They came to see that disestablishment could unleash a spirit of voluntarism that would boost the work of evangelism and spiritual renewal. They also enjoyed their newfound freedom to transgress the parish boundaries that had inhibited their attempts to promote revival. On the one hand, disestablishment led to an exponential increase in religious institutions, none of which was able to claim a legally sanctioned cultural authority. On the other hand, it deregulated the religious marketplace, enabling new ministry groups to flourish like never before. As secular pundits often point out, evangelicals have always excelled at marketing their faith. Disestablishment created a free market for religion in which evangelical entrepreneurs enjoyed unparalleled success.

The Christendom model of church growth began to collapse in this country during the Revolution and early national period. The last state churches to be disestablished were the sturdy Congregationalists of Connecticut (1818), New Hampshire (1819), and Massachusetts (1833). By the 1810s, though, these churches already housed a mixture of conservative Trinitarians, Universalists, and Unitarians—quite a smorgasbord of Christians—and hardly anyone believed their legal privileges would continue.

Indeed, disestablishment proved inevitable during the early nineteenth century. Many observers, then and since, have been amazed, even shocked, by the major shifts in church attendance that occurred within its wake. On the eve of the Revolution in 1776, more than half of the nation's churchgoers went to Congregational, Presbyterian, and Anglican worship services—and supported the legal establishment of their churches. By 1850, though, these denominations contained fewer than 20 percent of churchgoers, while evangelical communities predominated the landscape. Baptists and Methodists alone comprised over half of the nation's attenders. Dozens of other denominations seemed to be sprouting up overnight. In short, a democratization of religion accompanied American independence. All kinds of previously marginal groups—evangelicals, Roman Catholics, people of color, women—began to enjoy the new opportunities for ministry.

Most prodigious by far was the growth of the Baptists and the Methodists. Scholars estimate that at the outbreak of the American Revolution there were 494 Baptist congregations in the colonies. By 1795, this number had more than doubled to 1,152, and Baptists were poised to exert an enormous influence on the church of the next century. They proved most powerful in the South and on the ever-expanding frontier, largely due to their flexibility in forming rural congregations. The Southern Baptist Convention, today the nation's largest Protestant body, coalesced in 1845 to facilitate this growth. German and Swedish Baptist groups emerged at roughly the same time (in 1843 and 1852, respectively). By 1850, Baptists trailed only Roman Catholics and Methodists in size among America's dozens of Christian denominations.

America's Methodist Church did not exist until 1784, when it was founded at the historic Christmas Conference in Balti-

**Francis
Asbury.**
Courtesy
of the Billy
Graham Center
Museum,
Wheaton, IL.

more. Its founding leader, Thomas Coke (1747–1814), had been ordained by Wesley himself and sent to America to administer its Methodist ministries. Upon his arrival, Coke ordained another leader, Francis Asbury (1745–1816), the only Methodist sent from England who had remained in the colonies for the duration of the War of Independence (a war that Wesley himself opposed). Coke and Asbury worked together to organize the Wesleyan clergy, founding the Methodist Episcopal Church on a formal basis. But while Coke spent the rest of his life moving back and forth across the Atlantic, Asbury remained and played the leading role in the rise of American Methodism.

Born near Birmingham, England, to parents involved in the Methodist movement, Asbury moved to Philadelphia in 1771 in response to a plea from Wesley for help with Methodist missions. He quickly proved a tireless preacher and a passionate evangelist. He encouraged his colleagues to "circulate" widely with the gospel instead of settling down in more comfortable city churches. Practicing what he preached, Asbury toured the country restlessly. In fact, he traveled nonstop for nearly forty-five years, covering three hundred thousand miles on horseback, crossing the Appalachian Mountains more than sixty times in the process, preaching sixteen thousand sermons, and ordaining four thousand Methodist preachers. He had no home—literally—and once told an English friend to address all future letters to him "in America."

Asbury's humble example of selfless, circuit-riding ministry became tremendously important for the growth of Methodism. Much like the Baptists, the Methodists enjoyed their greatest numerical successes in the mid-Atlantic states, the southeast, and on the frontier, serving people often neglected by the older denominations. In an era when the United States grew faster than ever before or ever since—and when most of the growth took place to the west of the Appalachians—their rough and ready approach to ministry proved essential.[7] Thousands of circuit riders took up the cause of preaching in the country. Their work was grueling. They were poorly paid and even more poorly educated. They often lived out of saddle bags, slept out of doors, and died exceptionally young (from exhaustion and frequent exposure to the elements).[8] But they evangelized the country like no other group in the Christian church. As a result, the nineteenth century is often called "the age of Methodism."[9]

In 1770, fewer than one thousand Methodists lived in North America. Fifty years later, there were already more than 250,000. By 1830, the Methodist Church boasted nearly half a million members, and by this time, they were fighting among themselves over gospel purity. As will be discussed in chapter 6, the 1830s saw the rise of the Holiness movement *within* evangelicalism, which in the minds of many had lapsed into spiritual laxity. But even before the Holiness movement began to divide the Methodist churches, they had split over issues such as race, justice, and governance. In the 1790s, James O'Kelly led the Republican Methodist schism over unhappiness with Bishop Asbury's use (or abuse) of power. After the War of 1812, the Canadian Methodists organized separately. In 1816, the African Methodist Episcopal Church gained independence, as did the

Circuit rider.
Courtesy of the
Billy Graham
Center Museum,
Wheaton, IL.

African Methodist Episcopal Zion Church five years later. In 1830, the Methodist Protestant Church emerged from urban debates regarding episcopal oversight. The Methodist Episcopal Church South split off in 1844 in defense of an ardently southern position on slavery. Conversely, both the Wesleyan Methodist Church (1843) as well as the Free Methodist Church (1860) began because the Methodist Episcopal Church had *softened* on slavery.

Despite all this schism, Wesleyan Methodism continued to grow by leaps and bounds throughout the nineteenth century, bringing Arminian views to the mainstream of American evangelicalism. By 1844, the first year the Methodists topped the charts as America's largest denomination, they claimed 1,068,525 members, 3,988 itinerant preachers, and 7,730 local ministers. Needless to say, the impact was great. Methodists forever changed the shape of the evangelical movement, beginning with the revivals of the Second Great Awakening.

The Second Great Awakening and an Evangelical "Righteous Empire"

Despite the gains of the Great Awakening, by the end of the eighteenth century, many evangelical leaders had grown concerned about the spiritual life of the new United States. They felt that the churches had grown lethargic, they feared that the Revolution had bred an unhealthy interest in the most secular forms of Enlightenment rationality (which were often hostile to Christianity), and they knew that westward migration demanded a doubling of their efforts in the field of home missions and church planting. The United States, they believed, desperately needed a revival, a season of spiritual renewal to fuel the growth of the new nation. Thanks to the efforts of various evangelical leaders across the country, a lengthy season of revival is exactly what they got.

The very mention of the efforts of Christian leaders to spark revival will raise in many minds a question concerning the nature of the Second Great Awakening. Until recently, most scholars have cited the Second Great Awakening as a telling study in contrasts with the first. As the story usually goes, the First Great Awakening was, in Edwards's terms, "a surprising work of God" that was both preached and understood in very Calvinistic terms. The Second Awakening, by contrast, was an orchestrated event whose theology was Arminian in that it stressed the roles that sinners can play in effecting their own conversions. Inasmuch as this story is usually told by Calvinist partisans—who sorely regret the role of Arminians in the history of evangelicalism—it is plotted as a tragedy, one that accounts for most of the problems plaguing the movement ever since. But while it is true, of course, that Arminians played a role in the Second Awakening—that thousands of Methodists participated in leading the revivals and contributing to the development of their evangelistic practices—this way of telling the story is oversimplified. In fact, the Second Great Awakening proved tremendously diverse. It occurred in three major theaters, each of which was markedly different in doctrine and style from the others.

The first major theater of the Second Great Awakening was New England, where Edwardsian evangelists prevailed. In fact, the Second Great Awakening played a greater role than the first

66

in the Edwardsian enculturation (or cultural takeover) of New England. In the late 1790s, Edwardsian leaders such as Timothy Dwight (1752–1817), now the president of Yale, began to promote renewal among the young and in the region's key churches. By the 1820s, a major revival was underway, and by the early 1830s, nearly every church in New England—the Unitarian churches excepted—had been attracted to the New Divinity platform. Dwight's students led the way in spreading revival through the region. Pastor and activist Lyman Beecher (1775–1863) preached up a storm in his parish churches (first in Litchfield, then in Boston), promoting the cause of home missions wherever he could. Yale professor Nathaniel Taylor (1786–1858) taught evangelistic theology and preached revival in dozens of churches around New Haven. Most importantly, itinerants such as the strenuous Asahel Nettleton (1783 1844) tied New England's Christians together with a common, Calvinistic gospel message. Each of these ministers modified his New Divinity inheritance in ways that led to division among their churches. As the movement and its resources expanded exponentially, they began to fight among themselves over what it meant to carry Edwards's mantle into the nineteenth century. But they did so, to a person, in the service of revival, heralding Edwards's New Divinity—in one form or another—all the way.

The second major theater of the Second Great Awakening stretched along and to the north of the Erie Canal in Upstate New York. Known as the "burned-over district" for the frequency, intensity, and heat of its revivals, it was dominated by Presbyterians and Congregationalists (though Baptists and Methodists worked there too). Its leaders had roots back East in New England but proved less interested than their cousins in conserving customary forms of Christian faith and practice. More progressive in their outlook as well as in their methods of revival, they also proved to be less conservative in their Calvinism. Consequently, they raised the eyebrows of the Edwardsians in New England, creating controversy within the Reformed community.

The most important leader by far of the revivals in New York was the Presbyterian-turned-Congregationalist Charles Grandison Finney (1792–1875). Though he was born in Connecticut, he was raised in New York. He began his career as a lawyer but then underwent a dramatic conversion experience in 1821. The morning after his conversion, Finney encountered one of his clients, a local deacon, Mr. Barney, who said, "Mr. Finney, do you recollect that my cause is to be tried at ten o'clock?" Finney replied famously, "Deacon Barney, I have a retainer from the Lord Jesus Christ to plead his cause, and I cannot plead yours." He quit law and entered the ministry, studying theology with his pastor, George Gale (1789–1861), of Adams, New York. He was ordained by the Presbyterian Church in 1824 and spent several years as an itinerant evangelist in New York as well as in cities such as Boston and Philadelphia. In 1832, he settled down in New York City, first at the Chatham Street Chapel (Presbyterian) and then at the Broadway Tabernacle (Congregational). In 1835, he accepted a call to move to Ohio and serve as professor of theology at the fledgling Oberlin College, which had been founded by a group of antislavery evangelicals. He spent the following four decades teaching theology at Oberlin, preaching regularly in the First Congregational Church of Oberlin (1837–72), touring the nation as a revivalist, leading Oberlin as president (1851–66), and publishing *Lectures on Revivals* (1835) and *Lectures on Systematic Theology* (1846). By all accounts, he proved the single most influential evangelical of his day.

Finney taught (notoriously) that "religion is the work of man" and that revival "is not a miracle" but "the result of the right use of the appropriate means."[10] As a supernaturalist, he acknowledged that neither revival nor conversion ever occurs without the help of the Holy Spirit, but as an experienced revivalist, he claimed that these things do not occur without some human effort either. In the providence of God, *means* are used to promote revival. Grace is necessary, of course, but God does not coerce the lost or save the spiritually complacent. Rather, grace is that which persuades us of the truth of Christianity. It enables anxious sinners to pick themselves up by their own moral bootstraps. It is promised to all who seek it earnestly.

Finney also taught that "the state of the world is still such, and probably will be till the millennium is fully come, that religion must be mainly promoted by means of revivals." Human sin and its deadening effects "can only be counteracted by religious excitements."[11] Therefore, evangelicals ought to be doing all that they can to bring them about. In keeping with this conviction—that God spreads genuine Christianity not by expanding

Charles Grandison Finney.

Used by permission of the Oberlin College Archives, Oberlin, Ohio.

the bounds of Christendom but by means of convulsive awakenings—Finney developed several revivalistic methods he believed were most conducive to the arousal of spiritual fervor. Known ever since as the "new measures," though they were really not new at all, they included mass advertising, protracted revival meetings (i.e., meetings that lasted as long as the Spirit led), lay leadership, public prayers offered by men and women alike, and, most controversial of all, the "anxious bench."[12] The anxious bench was a pew placed at the front of the congregation where anxious sinners sat for prayer and special attention during the meetings. Finney's critics thought it symbolic of all that was wrong with his new measures and the manipulative approach to Christian conversion they represented. But Finney himself, ever the pragmatist, contended that it worked and that his methods should be employed by all who cared about the lost.

Finney's controversial tactics led by 1827 to a showdown with the leading Edwardsian clergy of New England. Nettleton, Beecher, and their colleagues expressed concern about the new measures. A conference was called in New Lebanon, New York, in July of 1827, at which the New Englanders hoped to curtail the excesses of Finney and his followers. In the end, however, the Edwardsians failed to suppress the Finneyites. In fact, the longer Finney defended himself, the more he impressed his opponents with his passion and sincerity. Ironically, he was preaching in Beecher's backyard just five years later—with the support of most of Boston's Edwardsian pastors, Beecher included! Clearly, Finney represented the wave of the evangelical future. Revivalism had become the movement's premier institution, and successful revivalists were now the movement's preeminent leaders.

The third major theater of the Second Great Awakening was the region of the Cumberland River Valley. If the Calvinists back East had cause for concern about the Finneyites, they had reason to dread what happened in central Kentucky and Tennessee. As a rule, the burned-over district was led by inconsistent Calvinists, people like Finney who had roots in New England but were more concerned with religious results than with theological precision. The Cumberland, by contrast, was led by avowed Arminians—either Methodists, who have always been Arminian by conviction, or Presbyterians and Baptists with Arminian tendencies that put them at odds with more traditional members of their denominations.

The best-known event in this third theater was the Cane Ridge Revival (1801), often called "America's Pentecost" for the amazing outpouring of the Holy Spirit there. It was a massive camp meeting, the culmination of the labors of several frontier preachers trying to meet the spiritual needs of isolated western settlers. Camp meetings first flourished in the early nineteenth century, quickly becoming a pillar of rural evangelicalism. They featured campgrounds where pioneers would meet for gospel preaching, Christian nurture, and lively fellowship. Wooden platforms were erected at multiple sites around the camp. The wagons and tents of the participants usually skirted the perimeter. The schedule of services consisted of a cross between a revival and a country hootenanny, with peppy, interactive preaching, folk music, food, and fun. The meetings typically commenced during the middle

70

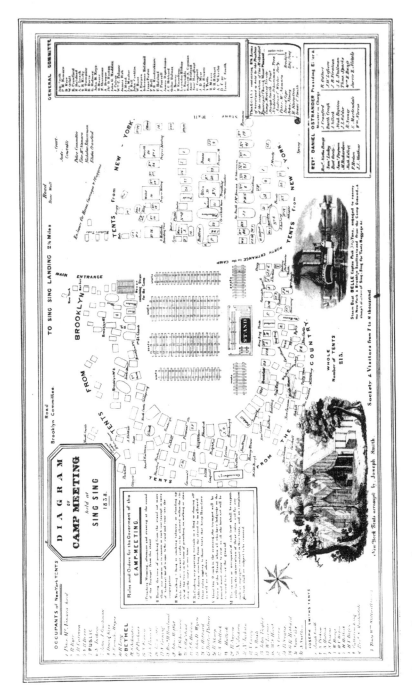

Diagram of a camp meeting. Courtesy of the Billy Graham Center Museum, Wheaton, IL.

of the week, lasted four or five days, and ended on Sunday with a special celebration of communion. They played a precious role in the lives of those without a church home. Thousands of people attended, making these meetings the most significant social events on the frontier.

The Cane Ridge meeting was held in Bourbon County, Kentucky, and was led by Barton Stone (1772–1844), an ecumenical evangelical who was born into an Episcopalian farming family in Maryland, raised by his widowed mother in Pittsylvania County, Virginia, and educated by New Light Presbyterians in North Carolina. Stone was converted under the Presbyterian preaching of two men, evangelicals James McGready (c. 1758–1817) and William Hodge (d. 1819 or 1820). He later crossed the Smoky Mountains and spent the rest of his life in the Cumberland, where he founded the region's indigenous Christian Church/Disciples of Christ (1832) with the storied Scots-Irish revival preacher Alexander Campbell (1788–1866).

But it was in August of 1801, while Stone was still a Presbyterian, that he organized the revival at Cane Ridge. Presbyterian, Baptist, and Methodist ministers helped with the gospel preaching. Thousands of pioneers attended. Estimates range from ten thousand to twenty-five thousand eager campers—and this at a time when the city of Lexington, the largest town in Kentucky, housed only 1,795 residents! Perhaps in part because of the size and scope of the meetings at Cane Ridge, the revival often got out of hand. Signs and wonders appeared all around, as hundreds of worshipers, slain in the Spirit, barked like dogs, jerked uncontrollably, fell into trances, danced, and shouted. Many easterners looked askance at such enthusiastic "exercises." But not many westerners worried. As Methodist preacher Peter Cartwright (1785–1872) noted of other regional meetings where bodily exercises occurred, they had an uncanny way of humbling even the finest cultured despisers:

> No matter whether they were saints or sinners, they would be taken under a warm song or sermon, and seized with a convulsive jerking all over, which they could not by any possibility avoid, and the more they resisted the more they jerked. . . . I have seen more than five hundred persons jerking at one time in my large congregations. Most usually persons taken with the jerks, to ob-

Peter Cartwright.

Courtesy of the Billy Graham Center Museum, Wheaton, IL.

tain relief, as they said, would rise up and dance. Some would run, but could not get away. Some would resist; on such the jerks were generally very severe.

To see those proud young gentlemen and young ladies, dressed in their silks, jewelry, and prunella, from top to toe, take the jerks, would often excite my risibilities. The first jerk or so, you would see their fine bonnets, caps, and combs fly; and so sudden would be the jerking of the head that their long loose hair would crack almost as loud as a wagoner's whip.[13]

Soon the rowdy western revivals and their rituals were regularized, as various Baptist, Methodist, Disciples, and even Cumberland Presbyterian (founded in 1810) groups arose to provide these new believers with denominational homes. The Cumberland meetings proved distasteful to many eastern evangelicals.

73

Their preachers were poorly educated, their methods were unrefined, their converts were rough around the edges. But they made a more practical contribution than any other single initiative to the sparsely settled Christians on the frontier.

As a result of the revivals, and in the wake of disestablishment, evangelical institutions moved to the center of American culture. By the 1830s, evangelical churches occupied the "mainline" of American Christianity. Evangelical parachurch groups performed the bulk of the social services offered in the United States. They even paved the way for the nationalization of U.S. public culture, organizing their work on a grand scale at a time when the Bank of the United States comprised this country's only truly national corporation, and the Post Office comprised its only national government agency.

Many refer to the first half of the nineteenth century in America as the age of the evangelical "righteous empire." Led by Edwardsians from New England but staffed by Christians everywhere, a host of ministry groups joined forces during the Second Great Awakening to impress the new nation with an indelibly Protestant character. They bolstered education, founding Sunday schools, education societies, colleges, and seminaries. They published tens of millions of tracts, books, and Christian periodicals. The American Tract Society alone, founded in 1825, issued more than six million items by the end of the 1820s. By the same time, the American Bible Society (1816) was distributing more than three hundred thousand New Testaments per year. To put these numbers in perspective, these two ministries—by themselves—printed more in this period than all the nation's commercial publishing houses combined.

Evangelicals assisted in founding special needs institutions such as asylums for the physically disabled and the mentally ill. They led a campaign to end dueling, which gained international attention on July 11, 1804, when Vice President Aaron Burr (Jonathan Edwards's wayward grandson) shot and killed a political rival, Federalist Alexander Hamilton, in a highly publicized duel in Weehawken, New Jersey. Evangelicals also led America's temperance reform, encouraging citizens to moderate their consumption of alcohol. More liquor was drunk per capita in the early nineteenth century than at any other time in American history. By 1820, in fact, the annual per capita consumption was *four times higher* than it is in this country today. Between 1830 and 1845, however, this rate was cut in half, and soon teetotalism became a badge of honor for evangelicals.

As we will see in the next chapter, evangelicals fueled the rise of the global missionary movement, the single most powerful engine for spreading the gospel abroad. Chapter 5 will show that they also contributed to the work of numerous antislavery societies. This list could go on and on. Evangelicals were involved in health reform, anti-Masonry, and ministry to Indians as well as to new immigrant groups. At times their work was self-serving, ethnocentric, even racist. They did not always serve those in need in ways that we would approve of today. But at local, state, and national levels, they labored tirelessly and effectively to flesh out the kingdom of God. Many believed that their work would usher in the great millennial age.

Men most often served as the public leaders of these ministries, but women provided the lion's share of the time, talent, and treasure. By the end of the Second Awakening, as the evangelical movement gained in prominence and prestige, it grew more socially conservative and curtailed the roles that women could play in public leadership. A surprising number of women had served as preachers, teachers, and evangelists during the century or so that followed the birth of the evangelical movement. Several hundred women, in fact, preached in the time between the Awakenings, though most of them came from sectarian groups like the Quakers (technically known as the Society of Friends) and Free Will Baptists.

Even after the Second Awakening, however, when women's roles were limited, literally thousands supported the movement's righteous empire. Indeed, its massive parachurch ministries could not have survived for long without them. A few still preached, and did so famously, like the black itinerant Methodist gospel preacher Jarena Lee (1783–c. 1850), the Holiness speaker Phoebe Palmer (1807–74), and Rev. Margaret Newton Van Cott (1830–1914), the first woman ever *licensed* to preach by the Methodist Episcopal Church who went on to shepherd the conversions of nearly seventy-five thousand souls. But most functioned in other capacities, either in leadership roles, like the teacher and theologian Catharine Beecher (1800–1878), the abolitionist Sojourner Truth (c. 1797–1883), and the temperance captain Frances Willard (1839–98), or behind the scenes, like thousands of women whose names are now forgotten but whose legacy in serving the cause of Christ will never be.

The explosive growth and cultural dominance of the evangelical movement did yield problems of their own. No sooner did evangelicals move to the Protestant mainline than some among them claimed that their movement was selling out to secular values. As we will explore in chapter 6, many constituents now contended that the movement had lost its sense of eschatological urgency. Its benevolent institutions, they said, had grown too bureaucratic. Their leaders had ceased to live by faith, to sojourn as "aliens and strangers" (Heb. 11:13) in a world that was not their home. In short, some critics complained that power had corrupted evangelicalism. They insisted that its members needed revival once again.

Virtually no one sought a return to the spiritual practices of Christendom. As the Swiss immigrant scholar Philip Schaff (1819–93) liked to emphasize—especially to Europeans—American Christians now comprised "a free church in a free state, or a self-supporting and self-governing Christianity in independent but friendly relation to the civil government."[14] But many wondered what to do now in the new American setting, where free churches had prevailed and religious dissenters had come to power—but where they had lost a pinch of their saltiness somewhere along the way.

Suggestions for Further Reading

Boles, John B. *The Great Revival: Beginnings of the Bible Belt.* Lexington: University Press of Kentucky, 1996. The best treatment available on the Second Great Awakening in the Cumberland River Valley and the South generally.

Brekus, Catherine A. *Strangers and Pilgrims: Female Preaching in America, 1740–1845.* Chapel Hill: University of North Carolina Press, 1998. The single best source on evangelical women preachers in the time between the Awakenings.

Conforti, Joseph. *Jonathan Edwards, Religious Tradition, and American Culture.* Chapel Hill: University of North Carolina Press, 1995. A fascinating survey of Jonathan Edwards's cultural legacy in America.

Conkin, Paul Keith. *Cane Ridge: America's Pentecost.* Madison: University of Wisconsin Press, 1990. The best brief introduction to the Cane Ridge Revival. Not nearly as comprehensive or original as Boles (above) but more satisfying regarding Cane Ridge itself.

Finke, Roger, and Rodney Stark. *The Churching of America, 1776–1990: Winners and Losers in Our Religious Economy.* New Brunswick: Rutgers University Press, 1992. A controversial account of the rise of evangelicalism in the wake of disestablishment. Finke and Stark overwork their market thesis regarding the blessings of religious competition, but they give a lively summary of the issues at stake in assessing what they call the "deregulation" of religion.

Fitzmier, John R. *New England's Moral Legislator: Timothy Dwight, 1752–1817.* Religion in North America. Bloomington: Indiana University Press, 1998. The best treatment available of Dwight (Edwards's grandson) and his role in New England's Second Great Awakening.

Hamburger, Philip. *Separation of Church and State.* Cambridge: Harvard University Press, 2002. A lengthy but helpful look at the separation of church and state in American history. Hamburger argues successfully that most recent applications of the wall of separation stand at odds with what the founding fathers intended and derive, most significantly, from mid-nineteenth-century anti-Catholicism.

Hatch, Nathan O. *The Democratization of American Christianity.* New Haven: Yale University Press, 1989. The most influential book written on American Christianity in the last twenty years. Hatch argues that a democratic revolution occurred in America's Christian churches during the early national period that reflected the revolution in society at large. This religious revolution empowered all sorts of believers—evangelicals included—who had been marginalized by colonial establishments.

Heyrman, Christine Leigh. *Southern Cross: The Beginnings of the Bible Belt.* New York: Knopf, 1997. A readable book on the rise of southern evangelicalism written by a critic working hard to tell a good story. Heyrman exaggerates the foibles of her evangelical subjects and the extent to which they accommodated to secular southern values. But her book reads like a novel. Even southern Christian conservatives find it hard to put down.

Isaac, Rhys. *The Transformation of Virginia, 1740–1790*. Chapel Hill: University of North Carolina Press, 1982. A fascinating history that deals with the powerful roles evangelicals played in Virginia's revolution. A nice complement to more standard treatments of southern Christianity. A bit technical for nonspecialists.

Marty, Martin E. *Righteous Empire: The Protestant Experience in America*. 1970; reprint, New York: Harper Torchbooks, 1977. The classic source on the nature and significance of the so-called righteous empire.

Mathews, Donald G. *Religion in the Old South*. Chicago: University of Chicago Press, 1977. The definitive survey of Christianity in early southern history.

Niebuhr, H. Richard. *The Kingdom of God in America*. New York: Harper & Brothers, 1937. A now-classic essay on what Niebuhr deemed the movement of God's kingdom in American history through (and in spite of) the social structures that tended to suppress its vitality.

Pelikan, Jaroslav. *Spirit versus Structure: Luther and the Institutions of the Church*. New York: Harper & Row, 1968. A learned treatment of Luther's experience with the tension between Spirit and structure and its role in shaping subsequent Protestant history.

Sweeney, Douglas A. *Nathaniel Taylor, New Haven Theology, and the Legacy of Jonathan Edwards*. New York: Oxford University Press, 2003. An explanation of Taylor's importance as the most influential—and controversial—American theologian in the days of the righteous empire.

Wigger, John H. *Taking Heaven by Storm: Methodism and the Rise of Popular Christianity in America*. New York: Oxford University Press, 1998. A wonderful book on early American Methodism. Especially good on the roles of circuit-riding clergymen in the spread of Christianity on the frontier.

Wills, Gregory A. *Democratic Religion: Freedom, Authority, and Church Discipline in the Baptist South, 1785–1900*. New York: Oxford University Press, 1997. The most sophisticated book to date on the rise of Southern Baptists.

As the Waters Cover the Sea

The Rise of Evangelical Missions

For the earth will be full of the knowledge of the LORD as the waters cover the sea.

Isaiah 11:9

Evangelicals care about nothing more than evangelizing the world. This has always been the case—ever since the Great Awakening. Indeed, evangelicals inaugurated the global missions movement amid the residue of the eighteenth-century revivals. They built its leading institutions, produced the bulk of its gospel literature, and dispatched most of its workers into the harvest.

Of course, devoted disciples of Christ have eagerly witnessed to the gospel ever since the glorious day of his resurrection. But as we will see in the pages below, something special happened after the birth of modern evangelicalism. Unprecedented numbers of people engaged in missions abroad, with the backing of an unprecedented evangelistic network. Literally thousands of Americans evangelized the nations, funded by millions of dollars of evangelical money. Soon the nineteenth century was known as the great age of Christian expansion. Many hoped that the twentieth century would become "the Christian century" and would witness the eschatological climax of world history.

No survey of the history of America's evangelicals would suffice without an account of these developments. Such surveys have been written, but as they ignore the powerful history of the modern missions movement, they fail to capture the driving spirit of its evangelical leaders. What follows, therefore, offers a sketch of early Protestant missions work, a description of the rise of evangelical world missions, and a summary of subsequent American attempts to observe and even complete the Great Commission: "All authority in heaven and on earth has been given to me. Therefore go and make disciples of all nations, baptizing them in the name of the Father and of the Son and of the Holy Spirit, and teaching them to obey everything I have commanded you. And surely I am with you always, to the very end of the age" (Matt. 28:18–20).

Early Protestant Missions

The earliest Protestant Reformers understood the Reformation to be a wonderful work of God to promote true faith around the world in preparation for the second coming of Christ. They thought the end of the world was near and that their job as Protestant pastors was to purify the church, restore its apostolic faith, proclaim the gospel fearlessly, and thus resist the final ravages of sin, death, and the devil. They favored missions, to be sure, in their pursuit of these urgent goals, but in their age of Christendom, Protestant missions often looked different from what we have come to know as missions work on this side of the Great Awakening.

The magisterial Reformers,[1] like their Catholic counterparts, conceived of missions largely in terms of what scholars call "confessionalization." With the help of the civil authorities, they sought to inculcate their confessional views within their jurisdictions, among a populace often confused by the spiritual turmoil of the age. By means of preaching, catechesis, visitation, and church discipline, they evangelized the newly Protestant regions of "Christian" Europe, training their neighbors, first and foremost, in the practice of *true* religion. Unfortunately for the cause of *cross-cultural* ministry, however, their regions were often ruled by people with little concern—or even capacity—to administer Christian work outside their borders. They were embroiled in a series of wars fought over Europe's confessional boundaries that would curtail the spread of the gospel for more than a century. Some of the leading Protestant thinkers also taught that the Great Commission applied only to the first apostles anyway, that God had *decreed* to spread the gospel after the apostolic age mainly by means of the organic growth of covenanted communities.

All in all, then, early Protestant efforts at cross-cultural missions work did not amount to much, at least not by the later standards of the evangelical movement. This is not to say, however, that such efforts did not occur at all, or that they did not occur outside Western Europe. In response to the international work of numerous Jesuit missionaries, supported by the Vatican's new and competitive Congregation for the Propagation of Faith (*Congregatio de Propaganda Fide*), many Protestant leaders feared the global spread of the Catholic Church and began to exhort one another to work for the spread of Protestantism.[2]

By the middle of the 1550s, Protestant leaders such as John Calvin were sending ministers to Brazil—mostly Huguenots,[3] like the Burgundian Jean de Léry (1534–1611). By 1559, the Swedes had begun to labor in Lapland. In the early seventeenth century, Dutch and English trading companies staffed their colonies with clergy, though primarily to serve their fellow European colonists. Peter Heyling (1607/8–c. 1652), a German Lutheran, served in Egypt and Ethiopia, where he worked as a preacher, teacher, and doctor for King Fasilides (1632–67) and labored among the region's ancient Coptic Christians. The Dutch Reformed engaged in missions work in several different locations—including Formosa (now Taiwan), Indonesia, Ceylon (now Sri Lanka), and Brazil—over the course of the seventeenth century. Gijsbert Voet (1589–1676), their best theologian, published the first comprehensive Protestant missiological work during the middle of the century.[4] Oliver Cromwell planned an abortive Protestant Propaganda College—to rival that of the Roman

Catholics—during the Puritan Interregnum. The Quakers also launched foreign missions during the second half of the century in both America and the Middle East (among the Muslims of Jerusalem and Constantinople). By the end of the seventeenth century, Anglican leaders had begun to establish permanent institutions for the spread of the gospel abroad: the Society for Promoting Christian Knowledge (1698) and the Society for the Propagation of the Gospel in Foreign Parts (1701).

The Puritans and the Pietists, though, undertook the kinds of work that paved the way for the modern missions movement. It was not until the Puritans' work with New England's Native Americans that the Protestant world projected an international missions plan on a grand scale and with monumental expectations. And it was not until the Pietists' work in the early eighteenth century that Protestant missionaries enjoyed a great deal of success.

The Puritan planters of Massachusetts declared that ministry to the Indians was the "principle end" of the founding of their colony. Of course, there were other motives as well for their migration to the New World. But many believed that Native Americans had descended from ancient Israel—from the "ten lost tribes" dispersed soon after the exile in the Old Testament—and that their salvation was a necessary component of the conversion of "all Israel" that would precede the return of Christ (Rom. 11:11–36).

With millennial expectations, then, they evangelized their neighbors shortly after rowing ashore. They never mounted a massive campaign to reach the Indians systematically, but the seeds they sowed continued to yield a harvest for decades to come. In the 1640s, Thomas Mayhew (1621–57), a Puritan missionary from England, began an evangelistic program on Martha's Vineyard. At roughly the same time, John Eliot (1604–90), known ever since as the "Apostle to the Indians," began his work along the Massachusetts mainland. He founded "praying towns" of Indians, preaching the gospel, translating the Bible into the Massachusett language, and teaching the Indians how to farm and trade with the English. Founding fourteen towns in all, he sent a few of his charges to Harvard in hopes that they would return and help him serve.

Some have argued that these and other Puritan efforts at Indian missions are pretty small potatoes when compared to their
stated goals. As Solomon Stoddard lamented regarding Puritan
work with Native Americans (in 1722):

> There has been a neglect to bring the Indians to the Profession
> of the Gospel. Something has been done through the Piety of
> particular Men, and at the Cost of some in Old-England; But we
> are reproached abroad for our Negligence. Many Men have been
> more careful to make a Prey of them, than to gain them to the
> Knowledge of Christ. The King in the CHARTER says, that the
> Undertakers did profess it to be their principal design to bring
> the Natives to the Knowledge of GOD. But we have very much
> failed of prosecuting that Design to Effect. . . . We have reason
> to fear that we are much to blame for their continuance in their
> Heathenism.[5]

Stoddard went on to wonder aloud "whether God is not angry
with the country for doing so little towards the conversion of the
Indians."[6] By the early eighteenth century, on the eve of the Great
Awakening, others wondered if this was the case as well.

Indeed, despite their noble goals and occasional gains on the
mission field, some of the colonists burned with shame for their
ill-treatment of the Indians. In addition to crooked business
deals and spiritual neglect, by Stoddard's day, the English settlers
were responsible for the deaths of many thousands of Native
Americans and the enslavement of scores of other Indian men,
women, and children. Of course, the English and the Indians
skirmished throughout the colonial period, but nothing placed a
damper on missions like the brutal King Philip's War (1675–76),
the bloodiest conflict in colonial American history.

The war was occasioned by the murder of one of Eliot's "praying Indians," purportedly at the hands of three other regional
Native Americans. Hostilities erupted when the English hanged
the suspects. Then their chief—King Philip (1640–76), whose Native American name was Metacom—retaliated, his Wampanoag
warriors looting the Puritan town of Swansea. In response, the
New England Confederation determined to go to war, securing
the help of other Indian tribes from New England and New York.
To make a long, sad story short, Metacom's Indians destroyed
more than a dozen English towns, and New England's armies

decimated the Wampanoag nation. Those not killed were sold into slavery, including Metacom's nine-year-old son. Metacom's head was severed, quartered, and distributed throughout the region. Now the Puritans could move through southern New England uninhibited. But needless to say, their Indian missions had been badly compromised.

The Pietists' missions proved more successful and certainly nowhere near as deadly as the Puritans' state-church ventures. Beyond their well-known work of renewing the Protestant churches of central Europe, the Pietists' best-known early mission began as a gleam in the eye of the Lutheran King of Denmark, Frederick IV (1699–1730). The Danes' South Indian colony, Tranquebar, lacked a proper Protestant ministry. Upon assuming the throne of Denmark, Frederick decided to supply one. Unable to locate Danish ministers willing and able to go, he turned to Halle for help six years later, in 1705. His new court chaplain, a German Pietist by the name of Franz J. Lütkens (1650–1712), suggested two eager students of Francke for the assignment: Bartholomäus Ziegenbalg (1682–1719) and his elder associate, Heinrich Plütschau (1677–1752). By July of 1706, these men had begun their work in Tranquebar with international support. London's Society for Promoting Christian Knowledge lent them aid, as did Boston's cosmopolitan Puritan minister Cotton Mather (1663–1728), a regular correspondent of Francke with a heart for Indian missions. The Tranquebar ministry quickly became the most successful Protestant post in all of Asia.

More importantly for the rise of modern evangelical missions, the *Moravian* Pietists commissioned hundreds of foreign missionaries, more than any other Protestant group before them. Indeed, by the early 1730s, they thought of themselves as a missions community. Their importance in missions history rests not only on the global scope of their gospel ministries but also on the fact that their ambassadors did *not* represent a Western territorial interest or a Protestant state church. Rather, Moravian missionaries were independent, international, and interdenominational.

Starting in 1732, the Moravians moved a spate of missionaries through Continental Europe, into England, to the West Indies, and onto the North American mainland. We have already seen the roles they played in forging social networks that undergirded the transatlantic revivals. They also began an exceptional ministry to the slaves of the Caribbean, founding the first African churches in the West. They planted churches farther north in England's North American colonies—in Savannah (1735), Bethlehem, Pennsylvania (1741), and Salem, North Carolina (1753)—under the leadership of Zinzendorf's assistant, Augustus Spangenberg (1704–92). These communities functioned as centers for Indian missions led by the likes of the ardent Czech evangelist David Zeisberger (1721–1808).

The Evangelical Advance

Not even Moravian missions, however, would come close to the size and scale of later evangelical ministries. Protestants had always sought to witness to the gospel and had capitalized on missions opportunities where they could, but the possibilities for witness expanded dramatically as a result of the multilateral Awakening yet to come.

Indeed, impelled by the momentum established by early Protestant missions and quickened by the supernatural force of their revivals, evangelical leaders organized the modern missions movement during the final years of the epochal eighteenth century. Like the Moravians, they surmounted older denominational boundaries. But positioned as they were so close to the end of Christendom, they enjoyed more freedom than their predecessors to found a broad coalition of "true" Christians concerned to evangelize the nations. They also completed a transition in missions methodology begun in fits and starts by early Protestant leaders, a transition from doing evangelism by means of confessionalization to evangelizing by calling people to genuine conversion that transcends all prior confessional allegiances. In short, they channeled the spiritual energy of the eighteenth-century Awakening into the service of what we have come to recognize as modern missions.

The Scottish minister Robert Millar (1672–1752), a Presbyterian pastor in Paisley, paved the way. Beginning in 1723, he published a hefty two-volume *History of the Propagation of Christianity* in part, as he maintained, "to move our Bowels of Pity for that Slavery and Thraldom to which the Heathens, who

85

make up so great a Part of the World, are yet chained by the Enemy of Mankind."[7] As Millar noted with excitement, "Christians in many Parts of the World seem now to be awakened with a more than ordinary Concern to have the Salvation purchased by Christ known over the whole habitable Earth." He prayed "that the Earth may be full of the Knowledge of the Lord, as the Waters cover the Sea."[8] But he lamented that Roman Catholics had bested the Protestants in missions. Throughout his *History*, Millar appealed to "the unwearied Diligence" of the Catholics, hoping to "awaken" his fellow Protestants "to a more serious Concern." He asked, "Shall the Popish Missionaries compass Sea and Land to make Proselytes, and we Protestants loiter, sit still, and do nothing?"[9] Millar, for one, certainly hoped not, and his own diligent efforts to chronicle the history of redemption through the spread of world missions succeeded in rousing Protestants to the cause.

One who heeded Millar's message was New England's Jonathan Edwards, who owned a copy of the work and echoed its call for Protestant missions. A prolific author in his own right, Edwards, as we have seen, inspired countless Calvinist ministers to promote cross-cultural ministry. For others, though, it was Edwards's example as a missionary—and missionary biographer—that encouraged a new commitment to evangelism. In 1747, Edwards promoted a transatlantic, evangelical concert of prayer "for the revival of religion and the advancement of Christ's kingdom."[10] In 1736, his congregation in Northampton had helped to found a frontier Indian mission in Stockbridge, Massachusetts. In 1751, Edwards moved to Stockbridge himself, becoming the leading missionary in the colonies.

But most significant of all for the rapid spread of Protestant missions was his *Life of David Brainerd* (1749), the most popular book that Edwards ever published. As mentioned in chapter 3, Brainerd ministered as a missionary to Indians in New Jersey (as well as New York and Pennsylvania). He was a protégé of Edwards, and he represented to Edwards, as to millions ever since, "a remarkable instance of true and eminent Christian piety"[11]—the ideal, outward-reaching, gospel-driven evangelical. Brainerd died of tuberculosis at the age of twenty-nine, drawing his final breath from a bed in Edwards's parsonage. But he had kept a strikingly intimate spiritual diary for years.

Edwards organized his *Life* around selections from the diary, and, though Brainerd served for less than five years on the mission field, Edwards's *Life* transformed him into a Christian hero. His rather ordinary tombstone in Northampton's cemetery became a virtual Protestant shrine, attracting pilgrims far and wide. His name was hallowed through the halls of the early missions institutions, and his legendary example of personal sacrifice for Christ—some have called it martyrdom—inspired multitudes to missionary service.

Most importantly, it inspired the English Baptists. Edwards's writings had been raising a global missionary consciousness in Britain throughout the second half of the century. His understanding of the will and his commitment to world evangelism had softened hyper-Calvinist resistance to such work. Scores of dissenting church leaders, most densely settled within Northamptonshire—a strongly Edwardsian county that raised such early missions leaders as Phillip Doddridge (1702–51), John Ryland (1753–1825), Andrew Fuller (1754–1815), and William Carey (1761–1834)—now championed the cause of international ministry. But it was the Calvinistic Baptists, such as Carey, who led the charge.

In 1792, Carey published his classic *Enquiry into the Obligations of Christians to Use Means for the Conversion of the Heathens.* The Anglo-American missions movement now had a banner around which to rally, one that emphasized its *duty* to cross the nations' cultural boundaries. Later that year, Carey, Fuller, and several other evangelicals launched the illustrious Baptist Missionary Society, the most influential evangelistic agency of its day. Carey himself sailed for India in 1793. Others followed in his wake. By the end of the eighteenth century, England's evangelicals sponsored a host of similar institutions for international ministry: the Methodist Missionary Society, formed in 1786; the London Missionary Society (interdenominational) of 1795; the Church Missionary Society (Anglican) of 1799; the British and Foreign Bible Society (interdenominational) of 1804; and the London Society for Promoting Christianity among the Jews (Anglican), founded in 1808 by a German Messianic Jew, the father of modern Jewish missions, Joseph Samuel C. F. Frey (1771–1850). As a result, the nineteenth century went on to witness literally millions of conversions to Christianity—both Protestant and Catholic—more than in any previous century. The modern missions movement was in bloom.[12]

Though the English erected the early international missions agencies, America's evangelicals sent the most missionaries abroad. Significantly, however, it took them a while to get underway. Not until nearly 1800 did the New Divinity men commence America's first indigenous societies for missions, and even then their organizations devoted themselves to what would later be called the work of "home missions." Both the Connecticut Missionary Society (1797–98) and the Massachusetts Missionary Society (1799)—whose efforts culminated in the larger American Home Missionary Society (1826)—promoted preaching, church planting, and the distribution of Christian books and pamphlets among the pioneers and Indians of the West. They exerted a weighty moral force on the formation of the new nation, but none of these groups made much of a difference overseas.

Rather, it took a group of college boys to expand their elders' horizons and to stimulate investment by Americans abroad. Their story is often told, but it bears repeating here, as it is crucial to the history of American foreign missions. In the summer of 1806, Samuel J. Mills (1783–1818) invited several fellow Williams College students to join him for prayer in Sloan's meadow, not far from their campus in rural Williamstown, Massachusetts. A recent revival at the college—which had become an Edwardsian school—had aroused concern throughout the community for world evangelization. Mills and his friends agreed to unburden their hearts in prayer for Asian ministry, but caught in a thunderstorm, they ran for refuge under a haystack, where they continued in prayer and committed themselves to service in foreign lands. This historic event has long been known as the Haystack Prayer Meeting.

These men continued to meet for prayer regarding the progress of the gospel. Two years later, they founded an organization for international missions. Known as the Society of the Brethren (1808), it was the first foreign missions institution in the United States. "We can do it if we will," read the group's Edwardsian motto. All of its members planned to travel overseas as missionaries, and at least three of them—Samuel Mills, Gordon Hall (1784–1826), and James Richards (1784–1822)—continued their training at the recently established Andover Seminary

(1808), the nation's first postbaccalaureate Protestant theological school. They stirred support there for their cause, attracting such seminarians as Samuel Newell (1784–1821), Samuel Nott Jr. (1788–1869), and the renowned Adoniram Judson (1788–1850). These men earned their school its moniker, "the missionary seminary."

In 1810, Judson, Newell, Nott, and Hall presented themselves for foreign service before the General Association of Massachusetts (Congregationalist). The following day they helped to found their country's first "sending agency" for international missions called the American Board of Commissioners for Foreign Missions (A.B.C.F.M.). In 1812, the American Board sent Judson, Nott, Newell, Hall, and Luther Rice (1783–1836), along with their wives, to found a mission near Calcutta. By 1820, the board had also made deep inroads into Ceylon (Sri Lanka), the Sandwich Islands (Hawaii), Palestine, and Native America.

Scores of missionary wives, as well as single female missionaries, received their education at Mount Holyoke Female Seminary. Founded in 1837 by the Edwardsian theologian and educator Mary Lyon (1797–1849), Mount Holyoke trained its students in liberal arts, domestic work, and ministry. Lyon sought to shape the whole woman. More importantly, she aimed to "teach nothing that cannot be made to help in the great work of converting the world to Christ."[13] Her school was nestled amid the rolling hills of western Massachusetts, roughly eighty miles from Andover—well situated for partnership with the latter school in missions. Countless couples left from these schools to engage in missions overseas. As the nineteenth century wore on, women enjoyed a greater freedom to serve in missions on their own. In fact, as a rule, they worked more freely with internationals abroad than they could minister to Americans at home. Schools such as Lyon's proved indispensable to their labors.

Among the many American missionaries whose stories bear retelling, two stand out as extraordinary evangelistic trailblazers. Adoniram Judson is the most obvious of the two. Many have reckoned him this country's foremost foreign missionary. After a celebratory send-off from the seaport in old Salem (on February 19, 1812), Judson spent four months at sea surveying what Scripture says about baptism. He disembarked at Calcutta on the 17th of June, continued his study of the Bible, and, before the

Mary Lyon.

Used by permission of the Mount Holyoke College Archives and Special Collections.

summer's end, had rejected his denomination's practice of infant baptism. He resigned his new commission with the A.B.C.F.M. (a pedobaptist organization) and was (re)baptized by immersion at Carey's mission in Serampore (north of Calcutta). He left for Burma the following year, won the support of American Baptists, and devoted the rest of his life to Burmese ministry.

Judson drafted a Burmese Bible and developed a Burmese dictionary. He was incarcerated and tortured during the Anglo-Burmese War. Upon his release, he worked to end the war by serving as a translator and assisting the British government with the Treaty of Yandabo (1826). He could not have accomplished as much without three gifted and gutsy wives—Ann (Nancy) Hasseltine Judson (1789–1826), Sarah Hall Boardman Judson (1803–45), and, nearly thirty years his junior, Emily Chubbock Judson (1817–54)—all important missionaries in their own right. He outlived the first two, but in April of 1850, he finally succumbed to a chronic respiratory debility. He died at sea after his doctor prescribed fresh air and a healthier clime. Sailors buried him in the depths of the Indian Ocean.

The second pioneer missionary who merits special attention lacks the celebrity of a Carey or a Judson. He died at the age of thirty-five, just eight years after the establishment of the A.B.C.F.M. But Samuel Mills played a greater role than any early American in generating commitment to the cause of foreign missions, and his service on behalf of several leading ministry groups helped to catalyze the age of Christian expansion.

Mills was born a preacher's kid in the town of Torringford, Connecticut. He was converted during his teens in a revival (1801) and went to New England's best schools. After providing spiritual leadership and promoting foreign ministry at Williams, Andover Seminary, and the A.B.C.F.M., he was licensed to preach (1812) and then ordained (1815) within the Congregational Church. He worked at first in home missions, distributing Bibles and preaching the gospel in the South, the Midwest, and among the poor of New York City. In 1816, he ministered at the School for Educating Colored Men. He also assisted in the formation of both the American Bible Society (1816) and the poorly named United Foreign Missionary Society of the Presbyterian and Dutch Reformed Churches (1816). The following year he went to West Africa, where he purchased land on behalf of the new American Colonization Society (1817), an organization founded to resettle freed slaves. It helped to purchase and settle Liberia (1822) with thousands of former slaves, to remunerate their owners, and to evangelize the region. Mills died a tragic early death at sea while traveling home from Africa. His body remains buried at the bottom of the Atlantic.

Former slaves are not always mentioned in standard histories of Christian missions, but colonization played a major role in American foreign missions. Its inherent segregationism left much to be desired. Many slaves would have preferred to become full citizens of the United States, but colonization did provide a number of black evangelical leaders with the means to inform the spiritual life of Africa.[14] Daniel Coker (1780?–1846), for example, became the first black American missionary to Sierra Leone[15]—an English colony in West Africa that, like its neighbor Liberia, was founded (1787) as a home for former slaves. Born with the name Isaac Wright, Coker escaped from slavery in Maryland, changed his name, became a minister, and eventually helped to found the African Methodist Episcopal Church (discussed in chap. 5). In 1820, he sailed to Africa as a Methodist missionary under the auspices of the American Colonization Society. Within three months he was the head of Sierra Leone's colonial government. He spent his life there as a leader in both the church and civil government, preparing a way for famous successors such as the ex-slave and Anglican bishop Samuel Adjai Crowther (c. 1807–91).

"The Evangelization of the World in This Generation"

Stories abound of such courageous, pioneering missionaries, people who spurred the globalization of the church. By the end of the nineteenth century, they had spread across the globe. American missionaries were stationed on every continent but Antarctica. They were supported by every denominational family in the nation. And they were poised to exert a massive force on twentieth-century history, one that would change the Christian church's center of gravity.

Significantly, more women than men contributed to this work. In fact, by the early twentieth century, literally millions of women filled the ranks of America's missions societies. In 1915 alone, over three million dues-paying members supported the work of forty American *women's* missionary societies. Many other women supported gender-inclusive missions societies, making the women's missions movement America's single largest outlet for Christian benevolence.

In the early nineteenth century, most women serving in foreign lands worked in the shadows of their husbands. As Mary Lyon once remarked of the ideal Mount Holyoke missionary, "She may promote the interests of the Sabbath school, or be an angel of mercy to the poor and afflicted—she may seek in various ways to increase the spirit of benevolence, and zeal for the cause of missions, and she may labor for the salvation of souls. But her work is to be done by the whisper of her still and gentle voice, by the silent step of her unwearied feet, and by the power of her uniform and consistent example."[16]

This is not to say that "women's work" was belittled on the field, at least not customarily. Men often categorized their work as being in a "separate sphere," but they also praised the "woman's sphere" as a crucial component of Christian ministry. Especially early in modern missions, women tended to express a greater interest in social and physical ministry, in fleshing out the gospel with Christian nurture overseas. They took an interest in education, in feeding and healing those in need, in cultivating a cordial context in which the men could do the preaching. An early nineteenth-century poem titled "The Missionary's Bride" communicated mainstream cultural expectations of such women.

> Who'd be a missionary's Bride,
> Who that is young and fair
> Would leave the world and all beside,
> Its pomp and vanity and pride,
> Her Savior's cross to bear?
>
> None—save she whose heart is meek
> Who feels another's pain
> And loves to wipe from sorrow's cheek
> The trickling tear—and accents speak
> That soothe the soul again.
>
> She who feels for them that need
> The precious bread of life.
> And longs the Savior's lambs to feed
> O, such an one would make indeed
> A missionary's wife![17]

During the second half of the century, expectations began to change as dozens of women's missions boards were founded. Women began to take the lead in shaping ministries for women. As a result, many of the brightest (and most independent) women in America volunteered for foreign missions.

Many mainstream missions boards rejected single women for service. Single women, in turn, began to establish boards of their own, expanding support for modern missions exponentially. Led by the likes of Lucy Peabody (1861–1949) and Helen Barrett Montgomery (1861–1934), they administered resources from and for America's women. As explained in the challenging words of a leading southern Methodist woman, "It remains for the women of the nineteenth century to do that which had never been undertaken before—that is, through the organization of her own sex into societies, to procure the means to begin the work of Christianizing the women in heathen lands."[18] Millions of women, young and old, were now responding to this challenge.

By the end of the nineteenth century, this new agenda for women's ministry had been captured in the popular slogan "Woman's Work for Woman." By the early twentieth century, the women's missions movement grew so large that it reached the peak of its global influence. It proved so powerful, in fact, that by the early 1930s, male denominational leaders sought to co-opt its institutions. They now accepted single women for assignments overseas. They put many other women to work on their denominational boards. Ironically, then, women lost control of the women's movement, but they continued to fund evangelical ministries all around the world.

The most consequential female missionary of nineteenth-century America was the Southern Baptist Charlotte (Lottie) Diggs Moon (1840–1912). Born in Albemarle County, Virginia, she went to Virginia Female Seminary and Albemarle Female Institute. In 1872, she left for China as a missionary, one of the first single women sent overseas by Southern Baptists. She worked for forty years in China, teaching children and evangelizing hundreds of Chinese women in both Tengchow and Pingtu. In countless letters and articles published in the Southern Baptist press, she challenged women to form their own female missionary societies and to follow her into a life of foreign service. She stayed unmarried to the end, struggling with bouts of loneliness. She also endured tumultuous times in her beloved land of China. Most famously, she survived the anti-Western Boxer Uprising (1899–1900), which involved a number of fierce attacks on foreign missionaries. By December of 1912, her chronic illnesses and regular bouts of depression overtook her. Her friends determined to send her home, securing her place on board a ship. But like so many early missionaries, Lottie died at sea—on Christmas Eve while docked in the harbor of Kobe, Japan.

Charlotte (Lottie) Moon.

Used by permission of the International Mission Board.

Southern Baptists like Lottie Moon have played an enormous role in the spread of evangelical foreign missions. Since the end of the nineteenth century, they have comprised one of the world's largest sending denominations, not least because of their annual Lottie Moon Christmas offering. Begun in 1888 with a total of three thousand dollars, this annual fund for foreign missions is now approaching one hundred million dollars. Thousands of Southern Baptist missionaries have served with its support. By this and other generous means, Southern Baptists have set the gold standard for missions.

Thanks to such herculean efforts, evangelical missions exploded at the end of the nineteenth century. In 1890, 934 Americans served overseas. By 1900, the number had grown to nearly 5,000 missionaries. By 1915, it exceeded 9,000, having increased almost 1,000 percent in 25 years. A new generation of leaders arose to supervise the recruits, building on the legendary labors of senior missionary strategists such as the Baptist A. J. Gordon (1836–95) and the Presbyterian A. T. Pierson (1837–1911),[19] both of whom inspired commitment to the cause of foreign missions with the premillennial doctrine of the imminent return of Christ (discussed in chap. 7) and a contagious concern for the practice of personal holiness (see chap. 6). By the early twentieth century, however, no one was doing more to promote the cause of international missions than John R. Mott (1865–1955), a Methodist layman and the most energetic organizer in modern missions history.

In July of 1886, while still in college at Cornell, Mott spent a month at D. L. Moody's (1837–99) summer conference in Mount Hermon (Massachusetts). The leading revivalist in America at the end of the nineteenth century, Moody sponsored Bible conferences in cities throughout the world at which he promoted premillennialism, holiness, and missions—all defining themes of the evangelical movement in his day. At Mount Hermon, with ninety-nine others, Mott subscribed a historic pledge: "It is my purpose, if God permit, to become a foreign missionary." He and the other "Mount Hermon Hundred" left the conference on fire for missions, persuaded their friends to sign the pledge, and thus inaugurated the so-called Student Volunteer Movement (SVM), named in 1888 and chaired for thirty-two years by Mott. A. T. Pierson coined its slogan (which became known as its watchword): "the evangelization of the world in this generation."

Both the SVM and its watchword inspired thousands of missionaries. The SVM alone enlisted well over twenty thousand students for missionary service. When it declined (due primarily to theological liberalism), its evangelical members founded an alternate missions group, the Student Foreign Missions Fellowship (SFMF), in 1936. Nine years later, SFMF joined InterVarsity Christian Fellowship (IVCF) and started what is now a triennial student missions conference, one that is named for its location at the University of Illinois. The Urbana Conference continues to carry Mott's passion for missions into the future, exciting thousands of students with a concern for global ministry.

Practically speaking, the SVM worked as the missionary arm of the Young Men's Christian Association (YMCA), another min-

D. L. Moody.
Courtesy of the
Billy Graham
Center Museum,
Wheaton, IL.

istry Mott served for most of his life. From his college days at Cornell—where he built its largest and most vibrant collegiate chapter in the United States—to his tenure as general secretary (1915–31), Mott invested forty-four years in the YMCA. He believed in America's youth. Moreover, he knew that they represented the future of evangelical missions. Even as an older man, Mott majored in ministries that attracted young adults.

Mott's career was so full and varied that it defies summarization. He led the World Student Christian Federation for over three decades. He chaired the World Missionary Conference at Edinburgh in 1910. He went on to rear its important descendant, the International Missionary Council (1921–41). He even worked as a founding father of the World Council of Churches, which named him honorary president in 1948. In recognition of his many years of ecumenical labor, Mott was awarded the Nobel Peace Prize in 1946. By the time of his death nine years later, he had traveled an estimated 1.7 million miles—almost always by sea and rail—becoming the senior statesman of global Christianity.

By the 1920s and 1930s, however, the missionary movement had come under fire from several quarters. A growing number of mainline Protestant leaders, and foreign nationals too, complained that America's missionaries employed imperialistic methods and promoted racist views in their evangelistic practice.

The modern missions movement boomed in the very period when America entered the international stage. As a result, the gospel was not the only thing America sent overseas. American politics, commerce, and culture often attended the Christian message. Many patriotic Christians who loved the American way of life—and who prided themselves on the blessings of their nation's "righteous empire"—often neglected the crucial task of distinguishing biblical Christianity from the rest of American culture.

Of the hundreds of missions hymns written and sung in the nineteenth century—both inspiring and informing missionaries and their converts—many symbolized this subtle but awkward tendency to package genuine passion for the spiritual health of people everywhere in a shiny, Western wrapper of cultural chauvinism. The era's most popular missions hymn, titled "From Greenland's Icy Mountains" (1819), expresses this tendency typically:

> From Greenland's icy mountains,
> From India's coral strand;
> Where Afric's sunny fountains
> Roll down their golden sand;
> From many an ancient river,
> From many a palmy plain,
> They call us to deliver
> Their land from error's chain.
>
> What tho' the spicy breezes
> Blow soft o'er Ceylon's isle,

98

Tho' every prospect pleases,
And only man is vile;
In vain with lavish kindness
The gifts of God are strown;
The heathen in his blindness
Bows down to wood and stone.

Shall we, whose souls are lighted
With wisdom from on high,
Shall we to men benighted
The lamp of life deny?
Salvation! O Salvation!
The joyful sound proclaim,
Till each remotest nation
Has learn'd Messiah's name.

Waft, waft, ye winds, his story,
And you, ye waters, roll,
Till, like a sea of glory,
It spreads from pole to pole;
Till o'er our ransom'd nature,
The Lamb for sinners slain,
Redeemer, King, Creator,
In bliss returns to reign.[20]

Sometimes the line proved rather thin between proclaiming the gospel abroad and condescending to correct the "errors" of backward "heathen" cultures.

Liberal critics usually exaggerated the failures overseas, but there was a kernel of truth in their claims. In response, many mainline missions ceased evangelizing, devoting all their labor to social and physical ministry. Evangelicals, for their part, kept on verbalizing the gospel, but even they began to modify their evangelistic methods.

The most confounding criticisms came from Presbyterian missionary to China Pearl S. Buck (1892–1973) and the Commission of Appraisal charged with producing the Laymen's Foreign Missions Inquiry, *Re-Thinking Missions* (1932). As an ex-evangelical missionary and award-winning novelist,[21] Buck commanded a lot of attention for her views. So when she criticized her fellow American missionaries in China and suggested that they relinquish their evangelistic ministry, she quickly became a lightning rod in the global Christian community. In 1932, when in New York's Hotel Astor she addressed her famous question, "Is there a case for foreign missions?" she did manage to answer with a (highly qualified) yes. Still, the case she made for missions sounded so different from the traditional one that she scandalized the churches—even before she left her husband, married her publisher, and abdicated her own career in missions.

The organization that did the most to generate change in foreign missions was the notorious, pan-professional Commission of Appraisal led by the Harvard philosopher William Ernest Hocking (1873–1966). The commission's report, *Re-Thinking Missions,* began with a stern reminder to readers: "The old fervor" for foreign missions has been replaced "in some quarters by questionings if not by indifference." Indeed, "problems of the utmost gravity face mission boards in nearly all fields. There is a growing conviction that the mission enterprise is at a fork in the road, and that momentous decisions are called for."[22] While summarizing the state of foreign missions around the world (paying special attention to Asia), Professor Hocking and his colleagues recommended several "decisions," hoping to help their churches with the revolution they thought was needed. They did pay lip service to evangelism but then went on to declaim:

> The Christian way of life is capable of transmitting itself by quiet personal contact and contagion, and there are circumstances in which this is the perfect mode of speech. Ministry to the secular needs of men in the spirit of Christ, moreover, *is* evangelism, in the right sense of the word. . . . We believe that the time has come to set the educational and other philanthropic aspects of mission work free from organized responsibility to the work of conscious and direct evangelism. We must work with greater faith in invisible successes, be willing to give largely without any preaching, to cooperate whole-heartedly with non-Christian agencies for social improvement.[23]

Few other Christians needed help decoding the bureaucratic prose. Hocking's commission had suggested that the future of Christian missions lay in humanitarian work, that evangelicals practiced a narrowly spiritual form of gospel ministry. "Men are to be saved," they announced, "not for the next world alone, and not out of human life, but within human life." They claimed

100

that most Western Christians had relinquished the idea "that sincere and aspiring seekers after God in other religions are to be damned." Most, in fact, now were "less concerned . . . to save men from eternal punishment than from the danger of losing" what they called—in an ironic, vaguely defined transubstantiation of terms—"the supreme good."[24]

Many conservatives responded to the commission with alarm and tried to distance themselves from the leaders of the mainline mission boards. The Presbyterian theologian J. Gresham Machen (1881–1937) led the way by founding an Independent Board for Presbyterian Foreign Missions (1933), a conservative alternative to his denominational board. The northern Presbyterian Church opposed the Independent Board, defrocking Machen for refusing to curtail it. Machen's supporters followed him into a new denomination, eventually named (tendentiously) the Orthodox Presbyterian Church (1936).

Now the battle line was drawn, and soon all kinds of missions groups fell into formation on the side of the old-time gospel. Older evangelical groups such as the Scandinavian Alliance Mission (1890—now the Evangelical Alliance Mission), the Sudan Interior Mission (1893—now SIM International), and the Africa Inland Mission (1895) aligned themselves in support of explicit verbal witness to Christ. Many new institutions also emerged, such as Wycliffe Bible Translators (1934), New Tribes Mission (1942), and Greater Europe Mission (1949), advancing traditional goals for their work in foreign missions.

Despite their defensiveness, however, evangelicals also countered liberal complaints about their methods with a stronger stress on what they called "contextualizing" the gospel. Evangelicals sought, in other words, to relate their faith and practice whenever possible through the cultural forms—the lifestyles, local customs, verbal idioms, and expectations—of the people whom they served. Many tried harder than ever before to distinguish the gospel from their culture, to "indigenize" the faith with the help of the nationals who received them. Making use of social science, especially the study of anthropology, they aimed, in the words of Paul, to offer the gospel "free of charge," to make themselves "slave[s] to everyone," to "become all things to all men so that by all possible means [they] might save some" (1 Cor. 9:18–22).

Consequently, evangelical missions continue to thrive today. In fact, it is not unfair to say that, since about the 1960s, evangelicals have comprised a large majority of North America's unabashed, evangelistic, Protestant missionaries. Evangelicals still relish tales of missionary martyrs such as the youthful Jim Elliot (1927–56) and his partner Nate Saint (1923–56), who with three colleagues died at the hands of the Auca Indians of Ecuador.[25] Their colleges and seminaries—most notably Moody Bible Institute (1889), Columbia International University (1923), and Fuller Theological Seminary (1947)—train hundreds of missionaries each year for international ministry. Many still struggle with ethnocentrism, but for the most part, evangelical missions boards and conferences—like the truly International Congress on World Evangelization held in Lausanne, Switzerland, in July of 1974—now feature non-Western leaders eager to help them understand that Christian citizenship resides in the city of God (Heb. 11:13–16).

Thanks to the efforts in recent decades of such international leaders, some of whom now live in America—like the Peruvian Samuel Escobar (1934–) of Eastern Baptist Seminary or the Burkinan Tite Tiénou (1949–) of Trinity Evangelical Divinity School—the heart of evangelical missions is heading south and east. Western embarrassment concerning the history of missionary imperialism; the growth of Christianity in Africa, East Asia, Eastern Europe, and Latin America; and the flourishing of missions in what is now the "majority church"[26] have led to a gradual displacement of American evangelicals as the world's most numerous full-time missionaries. In 1952, America still sent more than 52 percent of the world's missionaries, or slightly more than eighteen thousand people. Today, Korea sends more full-time missionaries than the United States. The Brazilians are catching up fast. And the Africans are sending a greater number of missionaries than any other continent did a century ago.[27]

One way of interpreting such developments is to assert that America's Christians have grown spiritually complacent—a generalization, to be sure, but one that holds true in many cases. Another way to account for them is to say that evangelicals, despite their obvious failures, have been used by God to expand the church into a global community, one that anticipates the scope of the coming kingdom of their Lord (Rev. 5:9–10). Of course, there are many other ways to interpret these demographic trends, and international ministry groups have miles to go before they sleep—especially in what they commonly call the "10/40 window."[28] Nevertheless, one thing is sure: Inch by inch, region by region, evangelicals are approaching a day when the work of "foreign" missions will be obsolete.

Suggestions for Further Reading

Anderson, Gerald H., ed. *Biographical Dictionary of Christian Missions.* New York: Simon & Schuster Macmillan, 1998. The single most helpful reference book on the history of Christian missions written in English. Edited by the former director of the Overseas Ministries Study Center in New Haven, Connecticut.

Andrew, John A., III. *Rebuilding the Christian Commonwealth: New England Congregationalists and Foreign Missions, 1800–1830.* Lexington: University Press of Kentucky, 1976. A helpful book on the roles that Edwardsians played in the world missions movement. A bit academic for most readers.

Bays, Daniel H., and Grant Wacker, eds. *The Foreign Missionary Enterprise at Home: Explorations in North American Cultural History.* Tuscaloosa: University of Alabama Press, 2003. A solid collection of fifteen essays on the cultural concerns of American foreign missionaries. The greatest hits from a conference at Wheaton College in 1998 titled "The Missionary Impulse in North America."

Clegg, Claude A., III. *The Price of Liberty: African Americans and the Making of Liberia.* Chapel Hill: University of North Carolina Press, 2004. The best history available of the colonization movement. Focuses most closely on the lives of Liberian colonists from North Carolina. Read this book along with those by Jacobs and Sanneh listed below.

Cummins, J. S., ed. *Christianity and Missions, 1450–1800.* An Expanding World: The European Impact on World History, 1450–1800, vol. 28. Brookfield, VT: Ashgate, 1997. An important recent collection of essays on the history of Christian missions, mainly in Europe, and their roles in early modern world history.

De Jong, James A. *As the Waters Cover the Sea: Millennial Expectations in the Rise of Anglo-American Missions, 1640–1810*. Kampen, Neth.: J. H. Kok, 1970. A crucial treatment of Protestant eschatological hopes and their roles in motivating the rise of Puritan and evangelical missions.

Elsbree, Oliver Wendell. *The Rise of the Missionary Spirit in America, 1790–1815*. 1928; reprint, Philadelphia: Porcupine Press, 1980. The classic history of the rise of American missions.

Hill, Patricia R. *The World Their Household: The American Woman's Foreign Mission Movement and Cultural Transformation, 1870–1920*. Ann Arbor: University of Michigan Press, 1985. An important but little-known book that shows that "much of the credit for generating the missionary revival of the late nineteenth century belongs to the woman's foreign mission movement" (2).

Hutchison, William R. *Errand to the World: American Protestant Thought and Foreign Missions*. Chicago: University of Chicago Press, 1987. A critical interpretation of the historical importance of the American missions movement. Written by a senior historian of American religious history at Harvard Divinity School.

International Bulletin of Missionary Research. In 1981, this journal succeeded the *Occasional Bulletin of Missionary Research* and became the most important periodical on world missions published in English. It is edited by the Overseas Ministries Study Center in New Haven, Connecticut.

Jacobs, Sylvia M., ed. *Black Americans and the Missionary Movement in Africa*. Contributions in Afro-American and African Studies, no. 66. Westport, CT: Greenwood Press, 1982. A somewhat dated but still useful treatment of black American contributions to Christian missions in modern Africa (especially West Africa). A nice complement to the books by Clegg (above) and Sanneh (below).

Kling, David W., and Douglas A. Sweeney. *Jonathan Edwards at Home and Abroad: Historical Memories, Cultural Movements, Global Horizons*. Columbia: University of South Carolina Press, 2003. A new collection of essays that discusses Edwards's powerful role in the spread of missions and world Christianity.

Latourette, Kenneth Scott. *A History of the Expansion of Christianity.* 7 vols. New York: Harper & Brothers, 1937–45. The classic source on the history of world missions. It has since been outmoded but not superseded.

Mason, J. C. S. *The Moravian Church and the Missionary Awakening in England, 1760–1800.* Suffolk: Boydell Press, 2001. The best book available on the influence of the Moravians on the rise of modern Anglo-American missions.

Neill, Stephen. *A History of Christian Missions.* 2nd ed. 1964; reprint, New York: Penguin Books, 1986. A readable, single-volume survey that might be described as Latourette light (see above). Written by a renowned Anglican missionary to India and historian of Christianity in India and elsewhere.

Robert, Dana Lee. *American Women in Mission: A Social History of Their Thought and Practice.* Macon, GA: Mercer University Press, 1996. Now the definitive history of America's female missionaries.

Sanneh, Lamin. *Abolitionists Abroad: American Blacks and the Making of Modern West Africa.* Cambridge: Harvard University Press, 1999. Far and away the best source on black evangelism in West Africa and its role in shaping West African social and political history. Read this along with Clegg and Jacobs (above).

Severance, Gordon, and Diana. *Against the Gates of Hell: The Life and Times of Henry Perry, a Christian Missionary in a Moslem World.* Lanham, MD: University Press of America, 2003. A delightfully written history of one of America's great missionaries and champions of social justice (on behalf of persecuted Armenians) at the end of the nineteenth century and the beginning of the twentieth century.

Shenk, Wilbert R., ed. *North American Foreign Missions, 1810–1914: Theology, Theory, and Policy.* Studies in the History of Christian Missions. Grand Rapids: Eerdmans, 2004. The best recent collection of essays on the history of American missions. Written by many of the leading scholars at work on this subject today. Part of a fine new series of books on the history of Christian missions published by Eerdmans.

Walls, Andrew F. *The Missionary Movement in Christian History: Studies in the Transmission of Faith.* Maryknoll, NY: Orbis, 1996. An exceptionally insightful collection of essays on the history of Christian missions by today's senior statesman of missions scholars. Walls is especially good on the relationship between the decline of Christendom and the rise of evangelical world missions.

5

Crossing the Color Line without Working to Erase It

Evangelical History in Black and White

My brothers, as believers in our glorious Lord Jesus Christ, don't show favoritism. Suppose a man comes into your meeting wearing a gold ring and fine clothes, and a poor man in shabby clothes also comes in. If you show special attention to the man wearing fine clothes and say, "Here's a good seat for you," but say to the poor man, "You stand there" or "Sit on the floor by my feet," have you not discriminated among yourselves and become judges with evil thoughts?

Listen, my dear brothers: Has not God chosen those who are poor in the eyes of the world to be rich in faith and to inherit the kingdom he promised those who love him? . . . If you really keep the royal law found in Scripture, "Love your neighbor as yourself," you are doing right. But if you show favoritism, you sin and are convicted by the law as lawbreakers. . . . Speak and act as those who are going to be judged by the law that gives freedom, because judgment without mercy will be shown to anyone who has not been merciful. Mercy triumphs over judgment!

James 2:1–5, 8–9, 12–13

The evangelical movement has suffered from the sins of racial prejudice ever since it first emerged from the eighteenth-century Great Awakening. While evangelicals did not invent the sins of racism or ethnocentrism, the slave trade, segregation, discrimination, or racial hate groups, literally millions of white evangelicals have either participated in or sanctioned one or more of these things, distorting their common witness to the gospel.

Consider the following statistics. Roughly eleven million Africans were coerced into bondage during the transatlantic slave trade. Half a million slaves were imported into the United States, but because American slave owners also owned their slaves' children, four million slaves were toiling here by 1860. In addition, half a million free blacks were eking out a meager living. Most of the slaves were grown men, but many, of course, were women and children. In fact, by the nineteenth century, 46 percent of them were children. In 1808, the U.S. government outlawed the importation of slaves. Hundreds of people, black and white, fought to free the slaves who remained, embroiling the nation in sectional controversy that culminated in war. In 1863, Abraham Lincoln issued his famed Emancipation Proclamation, declaring all the southern slaves "forever free." In 1865, the Union troops won the Civil War, putting an end to the system of slavery once and for all. But patterns of sin die hard. Racial discrimination continued, and evangelicals are still untangling themselves from this sordid legacy.

It is important not to forget the utter enormity of this evil or the extent to which evangelicals condoned it. But it is also important not to forget that evangelicals played a greater role than any other group in taking the gospel to the slaves and treating them as their *spiritual* equals. Paradoxically, while many leading white evangelical ministers owned slaves (Jonathan Edwards and George Whitefield), defended slavery (Charles Hodge and James Henley Thornwell), and preached to segregated crowds

(Charles Finney, D. L. Moody, and Billy Graham), some of these people also pioneered black evangelization, education, and even economic uplift. Many other, more progressive evangelical reformers played a major role in the rise of antislavery agitation. Further, evangelicals have contributed more than most white groups to the development of African American worship, doctrine, and practice. Conversely, African Americans have exerted extensive influence on the worship, doctrine, and practice of white evangelicals.

The pages that follow offer a brief, narrative history of the relationship between black and white evangelicals during the formative years of the evangelical movement, focusing closely on early white evangelical outreach to slaves and the subsequent rise of independent black denominations. In so doing, this chapter offers some needed perspective on the fact that most black Christians, though evangelical by many definitions, resist identifying closely with the evangelical *movement*. It also sheds some light on the inclination of most Christians, black *and* white, to ignore appeals for integration across the color line while at the same time embracing a surprising number of each other's cultural forms—in their homes, congregations, and public lives. Though evangelicalism has always been an ecumenical movement, its racial sins have often precluded the involvement of black Christians in its leading institutions.

Gospel Outreach to the Africans

Christian outreach to slaves began at a snail's pace. In fact, before the 1720s, virtually nothing at all took place that is worthy of mention in a brief survey such as this one. In 1724, a well-known clergyman, Thomas Bray (1658–1730), did establish an organization that made an effort among slaves. Best known as a founder and fundraiser for Anglican missions to North America—the Society for Promoting Christian Knowledge (1699) and the Society for the Propagation of the Gospel in Foreign Parts (1701)—Bray also started a mission to American Indians and slaves. Named the Associates of Dr. Bray, this mission sponsored teachers and schools for the dispossessed in England's colonies. The Associates achieved modest success in preaching the Bible to slaves and greater success in spreading their culture among non-Anglos in America. But it was not until the revivals of the colonial Great Awakening that large numbers of African slaves underwent conversion.

A major reason for the delay in Christian outreach to slaves was that slave masters viewed such ministry through thick lenses of suspicion. They shared a poorly grounded belief that, in the tradition of English law, Christian baptism freed slaves not only from bondage to their sins but also from bondage to their sinful masters. Consequently, slave masters resisted encroachments from evangelists. Many evangelists, for their part, only made the matter worse by insisting that baptism did not necessitate *physical* liberation but rather made slaves more obedient and submissive.

By the early eighteenth century, several colonies had passed legislation stating in no uncertain terms that Christian baptism did *not* grant slaves their freedom. But even after this legislation, many masters viewed slave ministries as economically detrimental. The evangelists, they argued, took the slaves away from their work and made them "uppity," independent, and ungovernable. In one of the tragedies of church history, many evangelists gained access to the slaves of such fearful masters with assurances that the gospel had few social effects at all, at least of the sort the masters feared. They emphasized such Scripture texts as Ephesians 6:5–8 ("Slaves, obey your earthly masters with respect and fear") and Colossians 3:22 ("Slaves, obey your earthly masters in everything; and do it, not only when their eye is on you and to win their favor, but with sincerity of heart and reverence for the Lord"). Some of them promised never to preach on God's deliverance of the Israelites from their bondage to the Egyptians. In short, the pact they made with these masters led to distortions in their preaching and wound up helping the masters more than it did the slaves. White evangelists desperately wanted to reach slaves with the gospel of Christ, but in the words of Rev. Peter Randolph, a former slave in rural Virginia, "The[ir] gospel was so mixed with slavery, that people could see no beauty in it, and feel no reverence for it."[1]

There were other barriers as well to the evangelization of slaves. Most slaves could neither read nor write, had little formal education, and found it difficult to follow the ministers' preaching. Even those who enjoyed some literacy resisted "book religion." In the early modern period, most West and Central Africans placed a premium on oral tradition and extemporary speech. The bookish nature of Protestant preaching simply did not appeal to them, and it was not until the revivals of the transatlantic Awakening that large numbers of Protestant preachers became dynamic popular speakers.

During and after the Great Awakening, however, all of this changed for good. Beginning in roughly the 1740s, America's evangelical preachers experienced unparalleled success in sharing the gospel with slaves. Many leading revivalists, from the Church of England's George Whitefield (1715–70) to Presbyterian Samuel Davies (1723–61)—not to mention countless Baptists and Methodists near the century's end—preached to audiences white and black, male and female, slave and free. Before long, black Christians themselves provided leadership in the revivals, offering exhortation and public prayer in racially mixed crowds. By 1800, tens of thousands of slaves believed the gospel message.

Relatively few evangelical preachers championed slave emancipation. Jonathan Edwards (1703–58) owned several slaves (we know the names of six of them). George Whitefield fought for the legalization of slavery in Georgia, petitioning Parliament for the right to employ slave labor at his orphanage. He claimed that "Georgia never . . . will be a flourishing province without negroes." Moreover, he purchased more than twenty slaves himself throughout his life. He even acquired a slave plantation in the middle of the 1740s "through the bounty of my good friends . . . in South Carolina," as he said.[2] Samuel Davies baptized hundreds of slaves in his brief, fifteen-year ministry (he died of pneumonia shortly after assuming the presidency of Princeton), but he excluded many others for viewing baptism as a promotion to "Equality with their Masters."[3] Clearly, then, evangelical outreach had its limits. Indeed, for most of these evangelicals, the gospel offered forgiveness of sin and eternal life in Christ, not a leg up in the here and now. For them, the benefits of salvation so far outshone mere temporal freedom that a compromise with slavery proved a small price to pay.

But such accommodation to slavery on the part of evangelicals established a pattern of prejudice that would plague them for years to come. Before the middle of the twentieth century, *most* of the leading white revivalists condoned discrimination. During the Second Great Awakening of the early nineteenth century, for example, many revivals were racialized, as black people were quarantined in segregated seating. This took place at Cane Ridge (1801), known as "America's Pentecost," by far the largest camp meeting in American history. It even took place at many services held by Charles Grandison Finney, who spoke out frequently against the system of slavery. Perhaps the most celebrated of all the nineteenth-century revival preachers, Finney allowed for segregation despite his progressive racial views. He deemed it inexpedient to allow black people to serve as church trustees, and he opposed more radical abolitionists for politicizing the gospel.

Both Dwight L. Moody and Billy Sunday (1862–1935) allowed for segregated seating at their meetings in the South, alienating untold numbers of African Americans. In the words of one black Christian, Moody's "conduct toward the Negroes during his Southern tour has been shameless, and I would not have him preach in a barroom, let alone a church." Another black pastor complained that Moody "placed caste above Christianity." The black abolitionist Frederick Douglass (1817?–95) compared Moody's meetings rather unfavorably with those of the noted agnostic lecturer Robert Ingersoll: "Infidel though Mr. Ingersoll may be called, he never turned his back upon his colored brothers, as did the evangelical Christians of [Philadelphia] on the occasion of the late visit of Mr. Moody. Of all the forms of negro hate in this world, save me from that one which clothes itself with the name of the loving Jesus. . . . The negro can go into the circus, the theatre, and can be admitted to the lectures of Mr. Ingersoll, but he cannot go into an evangelical Christian meeting."[4]

Even beloved Billy Graham (1918–) opposed discrimination slowly. Graham was never happy with race relations in his native South, and he angered many erstwhile friends in the summer of 1957 by inviting Martin Luther King Jr. (1929–68) to pray at his highly publicized crusade in New York City. But he did not desegregate his crusades for good until 1954, after the U.S. Supreme Court declared the "separate but equal" doctrine unconstitutional in *Brown v. Board of Education.* He seemed to symbolize to promoters of African American civil rights the "white moderate" approach to racial discrimination, an approach that King himself condemned in April of 1963 in his famous "Letter from Birmingham Jail":

> I must confess that over the past few years I have been gravely disappointed with the white moderate. I have almost reached the regrettable conclusion that the Negro's great stumbling block in his stride toward freedom is not the White Citizen's Counciler or the Ku Klux Klanner, but the white moderate, who is more devoted to "order" than to justice; who prefers a negative peace which is the absence of tension to a positive peace which is the presence of justice; who constantly says: "I agree with you in the goal you seek, but I cannot agree with your methods of direct action"; who paternalistically believes he can set the timetable for another man's freedom; who lives by a mythical concept of time and who constantly advises the Negro to wait for a "more convenient season." Shallow understanding from people of good will is more frustrating than absolute misunderstanding from people of ill will.[5]

Sadly, King was right. The history of evangelicalism is full of white moderate stumbling blocks, spiritual obstacles that reinforced its color line.

Yet paradoxically, and despite such undeniable moral failure, God has used the evangelicals to promote the gospel of grace among literally millions of African Americans. Ever since the Great Awakening, white evangelicals have engaged in Christian outreach to black people—never adequately but faithfully and consistently.

Some early slaveholders led the way. In a little-known letter draft (whose final copy has since been lost), Jonathan Edwards denounced the abuses of the transatlantic slave trade. In a better-known public letter, George Whitefield criticized cruelty to slaves. "God has a quarrel with you," he wrote to his slaveholding colleagues in the South, for you have treated your slaves "as bad or worse than brutes."[6] Whitefield persuaded some wealthy converts, the Bryan family of South Carolina, to become courageous leaders in ministry to the slaves. They never liberated their slaves, but in 1743, the Bryans left the Anglican Church to form the Stony Creek Independent (Presbyterian) Church, a congregation that received slaves as regular church members.

They denounced all cruelty to slaves and became such vocal racial reformers that their neighbors feared they would lead a slave insurrection.

The early Moravian evangelicals grew profoundly close to their slaves, engaging with them in Christian rituals of remarkable intimacy. This intimacy was later spurned by Moravians in the South. There were comparatively few black members of early Moravian congregations, but those who were shared with their masters in the liturgical life of their churches, experiencing a degree of racial harmony unknown to most other slaves. White and black Moravian Christians shared the holy kiss of peace, sponsored one another in Christian baptism, laid hands on one another's heads, sat and communed together in church, even washed one another's feet. After death, they shared a common burial ground.

Some other evangelicals opposed slaveholding altogether and engaged in dangerous and often subversive abolitionist activity. John Wesley (1703–91), for example, and his American Methodist followers opposed the system of slavery strenuously in the early years of their movement (though later on most Methodists backed away from such radical opposition, and their denomination split over slavery in 1843–44). So did several Baptist groups as well as numerous other sects, such as the Quakers, marginally connected to evangelicalism. Some New England Congregationalists (spiritual descendants of Jonathan Edwards) became important early spokesmen for the cause of abolition. Edwards's own son, Jonathan Edwards Jr. (1745–1801), along with colleagues such as Samuel Hopkins (1721–1803), published tracts and prophesied against the slave trade.

Out of the Second Great Awakening—the series of revivals that filled the first third of the nineteenth century—came a coordinated effort to evangelize, liberate, and educate America's slaves. Hundreds of thousands of them responded by placing their faith in Jesus Christ, and dozens of charitable societies emerged to minister to their needs. Of course, in American social history, this is the age of important leaders such as David Walker, Denmark Vesey, Nat Turner, and Frederick Douglass, outspoken black prophets who preached the most powerfully against the sins of slavery and racism. But white evangelicals, too, made a difference among the slaves. Though often much less bold in prophetic witness—and at times neglecting to witness altogether—they devoted countless hours and millions of dollars to help those living in bondage.

To take just one (rather conservative) example, the most important white evangelical educator of the slaves was a Georgian man, Rev. Charles Colcock Jones (1804–63). An ordained minister, Jones spent decades as a missionary to slaves. During the 1830s and 1840s, he wrote a catechism and teaching aid for slaves and slave missionaries, spending a great deal of time in the trenches preaching and teaching slaves as well. He came from a prominent slaveholding family, defended slavery from the Bible, and always argued that his work would not inhibit the southern economy. He believed that slaves had to be "civilized" before they would merit their freedom. Some have said, however, that he did more to improve the lives of plantation slaves than any other individual in antebellum America.

Most significant of all, the evangelical Awakening yielded a harvest of black antislavery reformers and black gospel ministers. Inspired by a scriptural commitment to the demands of divine justice, many black Christians began to raise their voices against the system of slavery and the evangelical faith that so often condoned it. Perhaps the most powerful testimony came from the ex-slave Frederick Douglass, who excoriated Christians for their complicity in this evil. "The church and the slave prison stand next to each other," he fumed. "The church-going bell and the auctioneer's bell chime in with each other; the pulpit and the auctioneer's block stand in the same neighbourhood." What is more, Christian ministries were profiting from the arrangement. "We have men sold to build churches, women sold to support missionaries, and babies sold to buy Bibles and communion services." Douglass summarized his concern in words that have haunted Christians since: "Between the Christianity of this land and the Christianity of Christ I recognize the widest possible difference."[7]

Scores of black gospel ministers emerged from the Awakening. Some served as pastors of predominantly white, northern congregations—Rev. Lemuel Haynes (1753–1833), for example, a black Edwardsian in Vermont. But an even greater number served among slaves and in black churches. This scandalized most nonevangelicals, who used the existence of black preachers to denigrate the revivals and worked to outlaw all black preaching in several states. Many black preachers and churches survived, however, and by the end of the nineteenth century, millions of African Americans worshiped on their own.

Slave Religion and the Rise of Independent Black Churches

By the time of the first U.S. census in 1790, approximately 20 percent of the country's nearly four million inhabitants were black. Most black residents were slaves working on large southern plantations, though some lived on small farms or in the homes of urban professionals. Most slaves worshiped, when they could, in the so-called invisible institution, the secret churches that met after hours for (often) illegal prayer and praise.

Slave religion is one of the miracles of American religious history. Usually unbeknown to their masters, and often in violation of orders and even laws against such activity, countless antebellum slaves "stole away" for secret worship in brush arbors, swamps, and forests throughout the land. They preached, prayed, sang, and danced into the wee hours of the night, more often than not after a long and grueling day's work. As recounted in Rev. Peter Randolph's autobiography:

> The slaves assemble in the swamps, out of reach of the patrols. They have an understanding among themselves as to the time and place of getting together. This is often done by the first one arriving breaking boughs from the trees, and bending them in the direction of the selected spot. Arrangements are then made for conducting the exercises. They first ask each other how they feel, the state of their minds, etc. The male members then select a certain space, in separate groups, for their division of the meeting. Preaching in order, by the brethren; then praying and singing all round, until they generally feel quite happy. The speaker usually commences by calling himself unworthy, and talks very slowly, until, feeling the spirit, he grows excited, and in a short time, there fall to the ground twenty or thirty men and women under its influence.[8]

116

Randolph went on to report on the persecution slaves suffered for meeting together.

> If discovered, they escape, if possible; but those who are caught often get whipped. Some are willing to be punished thus for Jesus' sake. . . . In some places, if the slaves are caught praying to God, they are whipped more than if they had committed a great crime. The slaveholders will allow the slaves to dance, but do not want them to pray to God. Sometimes, when a slave, on being whipped, calls upon God, he is forbidden to do so, under threat of having his throat cut, or brains blown out. Oh, reader! This seems very hard—that slaves cannot call on their Maker, when the case most needs it.[9]

Despite such treatment by their masters, slaves continued to gather together, often stressing Scripture texts and songs opposed by their white oppressors. They recalled Old Testament history, the Israelites' exodus from Egypt, as well as their crossing of the Jordan River into the Promised Land (often a symbol to them of passage across the Mason-Dixon Line). They spoke of God's justice in the biblical words of the ancient Hebrew prophets. They sang many poignant Negro spirituals that expressed their longing for freedom, here on earth as well as in heaven.

In one of their favorite spiritual songs, slaves identified with Israel and hoped for deliverance from their masters through their own Red Sea of salvation:

> My army cross over,
> My army cross over.
> O, Pharaoh's army drownded!
> My army cross over.
>
> We'll cross de mighty river,
> My army cross over;
> We'll cross de river Jordan,
> My army cross over;
> We'll cross de danger water,
> My army cross over;
> We'll cross de mighty Myo,
> My army cross over.
> O, Pharaoh's army drownded!
> My army cross over.[10]

In scores of other such songs, as well, slaves aspired to Canaan:

> Jordan River, I'm bound to go,
> Bound to go, bound to go—
> Jordan River, I'm bound to go,
> And bid 'em fare ye well.[11]

While most black people in 1790 worshiped secretly after dark, others worshiped publicly in more traditional church facilities. While most of these met either in mainly white congregations (usually in back pews or galleries) or in segregated black churches ruled by white denominations, some had by then begun to worship independently. These people founded what became the historic African American churches, the preeminent institutions in the development of black culture.

To this day, the vast majority of black Christians are Baptists, and this is not a coincidence. White Baptists proved most aggressive in gospel missions to slaves. Their spiritual dynamism, populism, and extemporary preaching attracted large numbers of Africans in the early United States. America's first independent African churches were Baptist as well. (The first independent black churches in the entire Western Hemisphere were built by black Moravians on St. Thomas, St. John, and St. Croix—in what are today the Virgin Islands—beginning in the 1730s.)

It appears that the first independent African church in North America was the African Baptist or Bluestone Baptist Church near Mecklenburg, Virginia (founded in 1758). But the first African church for which we have ample documentation was the Silver Bluff Baptist Church near Aiken, South Carolina. Founded in 1773 directly across the Savannah River and twelve miles east of Augusta, Georgia, its first regular pastor was a young slave named David George (c. 1742–1810). George belonged to a planter and Indian trader named George Galphin. When the Connecticut Baptist preacher Wait Palmer visited Aiken and led a revival near Galphin's plantation, George converted to Christianity. After Palmer left the region, George took over his work with slaves. No sooner had he done so than the American Revolution broke out, British troops invaded Savannah, and George's master deserted the farm. George eventually led his new church to freedom in Halifax, Nova Scotia. He planted and pastored several black churches in Canada's Maritime Provinces, and in 1792, he moved with 1,196 North American blacks to Sierra Leone, a new British colony of freed slaves. He settled in Freetown and founded an alehouse and the First African Baptist Church, which he served until his death in 1810.

The black revival near Savannah produced other ministers as well. Rev. George Liele (c. 1750–1820), for example, converted in roughly 1773 and two years later became the first *licensed* black clergyman in America. Liele's master, Henry Sharp, who was himself a Baptist deacon, manumitted him to serve as a regional missionary. After the war, Liele left for Jamaica, covering his family's travel expenses by laboring as an indentured servant, eventually for the Scottish General Archibald Campbell, the new governor of Jamaica who had earlier invaded Savannah for Great Britain. Liele earned his freedom and founded the Native Baptist Church of the West Indies. Before he left the United States, however, he baptized a slave named Andrew Bryan (1737–1812), who quickly became the most important black church leader in Savannah. Bryan founded in 1788 the First African Baptist Church in Savannah. He suffered a whipping from local whites for this unauthorized activity, but he won the sympathy of his master, received ordination to the ministry, acquired his freedom, and went on to found two other local African churches. By 1802, Bryan's First Church boasted 850 members.

As a result of this gospel labor, no fewer than ten independent black churches existed in the United States by the end of the eighteenth century. By the end of the Civil War, there were no fewer than 205. Many more no doubt existed for which no records survive. Baptists are fiercely independent and frequently nondenominational, but some black Baptists formed associations throughout the nineteenth century. The first major black Baptist denomination arose in 1895 from a merger of three, smaller African American ministry groups: the Foreign Mission Baptist Convention of 1880, the American National Baptist Convention of 1886, and the Baptist National Education Convention of 1893. Their merger yielded the National Baptist Convention, U.S.A., Inc., to this day the largest black denomination in the world.

The most important early leader of the National Baptist Church was an ex-slave by the name of Elias C. Morris (1855–1922). Converted in 1874 and called to preach the following year, Morris served as pastor of the Centennial Baptist Church in Helena, Arkansas, from 1879 until his death forty-three years later. A lifelong churchman and educator, Morris proved a natural choice to lead the National Baptist Convention. Elected in 1895 to serve as its founding president, he stayed at the helm until his death in September of 1922.

Though the National Baptist Church remains the world's largest black denomination, it has endured two major schisms since the early twentieth century. The first took place in 1915, when the head of the National Baptist Publishing Board, Rev. R. H. Boyd (1843–1922), withdrew his board from the larger National Baptist Convention. Following a protracted battle with Morris over control of black Baptist resources, Boyd founded the separate National Baptist Convention of America.

The second schism occurred not over a financial tug-of-war but over the denomination's approach to civil rights. Joseph H. Jackson (1900–1990) ran the National Baptist Convention, U.S.A. from 1953 to 1982—during the heyday of the movement for African American civil rights. He encouraged black Baptists to protest less and spend more time producing the goods and services needed to improve their standard of living. "Protest has its place in our racial struggle," he would say, "but we must go from protest to production."[12] This led to a rift with Rev. Martin Luther King Jr. and other Baptists working to mobilize black Christians for political activism. A debate took place within the convention over the length of the president's tenure. King and his colleagues sought a new president who would adopt a more aggressive style of political leadership. When they failed to replace Jackson, they left the National Baptist Convention and formed the Progressive National Baptist Convention, Inc. (1961).

Today, there are many other independent black denominations, but in addition to the three Baptist bodies described above, four others (described below) are usually categorized by scholars as "historic" black churches. All seven denominations have ties to the broader evangelical movement, but for reasons that should be clear at this point in the survey of their histories, few of their members feel comfortable aligning with white evangelicals. For reasons much harder to fathom, most white Christian leaders (not to mention the rank and file within their churches) remain largely ignorant of these historic African American denominations, despite the fact that they comprise well over twenty million members.[13] Both white and black Christians desperately need to hear their stories.

Though the Baptists founded the first independent black churches in America, the Methodists founded the first independent black denominations. And though Rev. Peter Spencer (1782–1843) founded the first such denomination—in Dover, Delaware, in 1813, eventually named the Union American Methodist Episcopal Church—it was Rev. Richard Allen (1760–1831) who founded the first *permanent* black denomination in the country, the historic African Methodist Episcopal Church of 1816.

Born into slavery in Philadelphia, Allen was born again in Delaware at the age of seventeen (he had been sold to another master). He soon began preaching on his plantation as well as in local Methodist churches, persuading many, including his master, to convert to Christianity. He purchased his freedom, received a license to preach in 1783, and traveled the mid-Atlantic states as an itinerant Methodist minister, performing odd jobs to pay the bills. He soon garnered a reputation, gained the support of leading Methodists such as Rev. Francis Asbury (1745–1816), and even attended the storied Christmas Conference of 1784, which gave birth to the predominantly white Methodist Episcopal Church.

In 1786, Allen returned to Philadelphia and joined St. George's Methodist Church. He led prayer and study services there for the city's African Methodists, attracting dozens of new black members to the church, which raised the church's racial tensions. St. George's leadership responded by enforcing racial segregation at its Sunday worship services. In November of 1787, this racist policy came to a boil. Allen himself described what happened in his spiritual autobiography:

> A number of us usually attended St. George's church in Fourth street; and when the colored people began to get numerous in attending the church, they moved us from the seats we usually sat on, and placed us around the wall, and on Sabbath morning we went to church and the sexton stood at the door, and told us to

go in the gallery. He told us to go, and we would see where to sit. We expected to take the seats over the ones we formerly occupied below, not knowing any better. We took those seats. Meeting had begun, and they were nearly done singing, and just as we got to the seats, the elder said, "Let us pray." We had not been long upon our knees before I heard considerable scuffling and low talking. I raised my head up and saw one of the trustees . . . having hold of the Rev. Absalom Jones [another black leader at St. George's], pulling him up off of his knees, and saying, "You must get up—you must not kneel here." Mr. Jones replied, "Wait until prayer is over." [The trustee] said "No, you must get up now, or I will call for aid and force you away." Mr. Jones said, "Wait until prayer is over, and I will get up and trouble you no more." With that he beckoned to one of the other trustees . . . to come to his assistance. He came, and went to William White to pull him up. By this time prayer was over, and we all went out of the church in a body, and they were no more plagued with us in the church.[14]

The offended group of black Methodists soon began to meet on their own. Some formed a black Episcopal church, but Allen and most of the others, being Methodists by conviction, grew dissatisfied with this option and in 1794 founded another Methodist church called the Bethel African Methodist Episcopal Church, or "Mother Bethel." Bishop Asbury, by now the leading Methodist in America, presided at the church's dedication.

For the next twenty-two years, Allen worked toward the legal independence of Mother Bethel from the white Methodist church. Local white Methodist leaders resisted his calls for black autonomy, but in 1799, Bishop Asbury ordained him into the Methodist ministry. Then in 1816, after a protracted legal battle, the African Methodist Episcopal Church became independent. Several other black Methodist groups joined the new denomination, and Allen himself was consecrated—again, by a sympathetic Asbury—to serve as the church's founding bishop.

Just five years later, the second historic African Methodist denomination emerged under similar circumstances. The African Methodist Episcopal Zion Church began in New York City in response to discrimination suffered in local white Methodist churches. Led by a former slave and shoemaker, Rev. James Varick (c. 1750–1827), a group of disgruntled black worshipers had in 1796 walked out of the John's Street Methodist Church of New York City. By 1800, this group was worshiping in its own church facility, Zion Chapel, under the preaching of Rev. William Stillwell (a white Methodist pastor) and with the blessing of Bishop Asbury. None of the region's white bishops—in either the Methodist Episcopal Church or the (Anglican) Protestant Episcopal Church—would ordain their ruling elders. In 1821, therefore, when local white Methodists attempted to tighten their grip on Zion Chapel, Varick and other black leaders at Zion took matters into their own hands. They ordained their own elders and formed their own denomination, along with other black Methodist groups in New Haven, Newark, and Philadelphia. Richard Allen encouraged this group to join his own denomination, but fearing the loss of their self-rule, they instead elected Varick to serve as their new denomination's bishop.

The third historic black Methodist church was founded much later, in 1870, by the newly freed slaves of the southern Methodists. Since 1844, the predominantly white Methodist Church had been divided, North and South, largely over the issue of slavery. At the end of the Civil War, the southern Methodists (officially named the Methodist Episcopal Church, South) were required by law to free their slaves. Rather than integrate them into their own white Methodist congregations, they helped them found their own, segregated black denomination. Thus, the Colored (later Christian) Methodist Episcopal Church began. Senior bishop Robert Paine of the Southern Methodist Episcopal Church consecrated Rev. William H. Miles and Rev. Richard H. Vanderhorst as its founding bishops at a ceremony in Jackson, Tennessee.

The Church of God in Christ is the first and largest African American Pentecostal denomination. Like the rest of Pentecostalism (discussed in chap. 6), it grew out of the so-called Holiness movement of nineteenth-century evangelicalism, a movement committed to the promotion of the power of the Holy Spirit for victorious Christian living. In 1895, two years after Charles H. Mason (1866–1961) experienced entire sanctification along the lines of the Holiness movement, he left his local Baptist church and founded a new church in a cotton gin shed in Lexington, Mississippi. He hoped to attract a congregation that respected the importance of entire sanctification and empowerment by the Spirit for supernatural Christian ministry. Soon he was joined by a Baptist pastor in nearby Jackson, Mississippi, Charles Price

Staff of the Church of God in Christ. Charles H. Mason is located front center.
Used by permission of the Flower Pentecostal Heritage Center.

Jones (1865–1949), who shared his passion for radical Holiness. Jones started a Holiness magazine (*Truth*) and, together with Mason, called a conference of like-minded African Americans. These Christians decided at the conference to found a new denomination called (eventually) the Church of God in Christ.

Over the course of the next several years, Mason and company made spiritual progress. But Mason, especially, grew frustrated that his group remained unable to heal the sick or cast out demons. In fact, he began to fear that his group had not been completely filled with the Spirit. In 1906, therefore, when he learned of the great Azusa Street revival—a series of interracial meetings held in Los Angeles, led by a black man named William J. Seymour (1870–1922), at which many Christians received special gifts of the Holy Spirit (most notably, the ability to speak in tongues)—Mason went to check it out. He came back claiming that he, too, had received the baptism in the Spirit along

William J. Seymour and Jennie Moor Seymour.

Used by permission of the Flower Pentecostal Heritage Center.

Azusa Street. Used by permission of the Flower Pentecostal Heritage Center.

with the gift of speaking in tongues. He said that the Church of God in Christ should join the Pentecostal movement (which distinguished itself from the Holiness movement by insisting on the necessity of the special gifts of the Spirit, most importantly glossolalia). Jones resisted Mason's new teaching, and the denomination split, Jones leaving to form the smaller Church of Christ (Holiness). Mason became the most powerful leader of the Church of God in Christ, and he made it a Pentecostal body. He served as its general overseer for half a century until his death in the fall of 1961.

African American Christian Practice and the Evangelical Movement

Scholars have debated for decades the extent to which African cultural traits have made their way into black Christianity and, through America's black churches, into the evangelical movement. These debates are as complex as the African cultures they represent and cannot be summarized adequately in a chapter such as this. Moreover, a comprehensive view of modern evangelical culture requires an equally detailed look at its other racial and ethnic roots (not least in the peculiarities of its European cultures). Nonetheless, a brief survey of the debate over African influence can inform an estimation of the culture of evangelicalism, its racial history, and the traffic across its color line.

On the one hand, some have argued that a sizeable number of Africanisms have survived in African American cultural life. The early modern African cultures from which most American slaves were captured included both animism and spiritualism—the belief that spirits suffuse the natural world and shape the course of events and that special people can channel these spirits and harness their power for social welfare. It is no coincidence, then, that black Pentecostals developed a doctrine of the anointing of God's Spirit strikingly similar to some of the African notions of spirit possession in humans. It is also salient that so many blacks enrolled in Baptist churches, given that African water cults often exorcized evil spirits by submerging possessed people in bodies of water. Most significantly, there are resemblances between African rites such as the ring shout—in which participants sang antiphonally, clapped, and danced in a circle or ring—and the dynamic and communal liturgical rites of many black churches.

On the other hand, many argue that these are merely coincidences, that there are sources in Christian tradition for these and related black Christian practices, and that white slaveholders largely succeeded in keeping slaves from hanging on to their African cultural heritage. First of all, these scholars argue, most of the slaves imported from Africa were young, single men, the sort of people usually least interested in transmitting their culture to others. After purchasing slaves, moreover, many masters sought deliberately to destroy their cultural memories, splitting their families, selling their children, and banning the use of their native languages. Many "broke in" or "seasoned" new slaves by isolating them from their peers, immersing them in plantation culture, micro-managing their lives, in short doing everything they could to keep the slaves from thinking of home. The result was what one scholar has called an "African spiritual holocaust."[15]

Sorting out this disagreement is often rather tricky business. It is nearly impossible to trace—at least with a high degree of accuracy—the transmission of African cultural traits through slaves to the black churches. Even if we could, the implications of this knowledge would be contested by black leaders and other interested observers. Most do not want to attribute black church culture solely to either the outreach efforts of white evangelicals or the pagan cultures of early modern Africa. It is important to most black Christians *both* to make good on their African heritage (demonstrating that Christianity is not simply a "white man's religion") *and* to maintain the best traditions of orthodox, biblical Christianity.

In the end, most experts agree that *somehow* African American Protestantism evolved as a special hybrid of black culture and international evangelicalism. Rooted deeply in the Bible and empowered by the Spirit, black faith was facilitated initially by evangelical witness. For better and for worse, then, black and white evangelical Christians have been knit together with yarns from a common spiritual ancestry. White evangelicals first announced the gospel to those they had enslaved, providing the means of grace for Africans in exile. In turn, black Christians

A plantation burial worship service. Used by permission of the Historic New Orleans Collection.

developed their own ecclesiastical traditions, improving on the message they heard and returning significant contributions to the evangelical movement. The Africans' full-bodied, improvisational, communal worship and praise; their dynamic preaching methods; their commitment to biblical justice; even dozens of their spirituals have leavened the evangelical movement here and abroad.

In recent years, moreover, a small but significant group of black leaders has embraced the term *evangelical,* forging ties with the broader evangelical movement. Through African American ministry groups such as the National Black Evangelical Association (founded in 1963) and the ministries of black clergy such as John Perkins (1930–), E. V. Hill (1933–2003), Tom Skinner (1942–94), and T. D. Jakes (1957–), a growing number of black Christians are making connections to evangelicalism while retaining their allegiances to African American culture.

To this day, only 5.5 percent of churches in the United States comprise an interracial membership. Both whites and blacks have crossed the color line, but few have worked hard to erase it. As I have tried to make clear, this is understandable, but from a biblical point of view, it is wrong. Time will tell whether evangelicals will integrate their movement before they cross the Jordan River together to enter the Promised Land.

Suggestions for Further Reading

Berlin, Ira. *Generations of Captivity: A History of African-American Slaves.* Cambridge: Harvard University Press, 2003. The best current history of American slavery.

Davis, David Brion. *In the Image of God: Religion, Moral Values, and Our Heritage of Slavery.* New Haven: Yale University Press, 2001. An insightful, accessible collection of essays written by this country's leading historian of global slavery. Especially useful on the international context of American slavery.

Deyoung, Curtiss Paul, Michael O. Emerson, George Yancey, and Karen Chai Kim. *United By Faith: The Multiracial Congregation as an Answer to the Problem of Race.* New York: Oxford University Press, 2003. A companion to *Divided by Faith* (below), this volume offers an engaging Christian argument in support of multiracial churches.

Emerson, Michael O., and Christian Smith. *Divided by Faith: Evangelical Religion and the Problem of Race in America.* New York: Oxford University Press, 2000. A poignant portrayal of current evangelical attitudes about race and the role these attitudes play in the racialization of American society.

Frey, Sylvia, and Betty Wood. *Come Shouting to Zion: African American Protestantism in the American South and British Caribbean to 1830.* Chapel Hill: University of North Carolina Press, 1998. The most competent recent history of black Protestantism in the early American South. This is a specialized academic study that may prove forbidding to some readers.

Fulop, Timothy E., and Albert J. Raboteau, eds. *African-American Religion: Interpretive Essays in History and Culture.* New York: Routledge, 1997. The best collection of essays ever assembled on African American religious history. A fine sampling of the most important recent scholarship on the subject.

Higginbotham, Evelyn Brooks. *Righteous Discontent: The Women's Movement in the Black Baptist Church, 1880–1920.* Cambridge: Harvard University Press, 1993. An excellent history of the efforts of mainly National Baptist women to serve their churches and make them centers of social change.

Juster, Susan, and Lisa MacFarlane, eds. *A Mighty Baptism: Race, Gender, and the Creation of American Protestantism.* Ithaca, NY: Cornell University Press, 1996. A collection of essays most helpful on the relationship between race and gender in American religious history.

Lincoln, C. Eric, and Lawrence H. Mamiya. *The Black Church in the African American Experience.* Durham: Duke University Press, 1990. The standard textbook on African American church history.

Murphy, Larry G., ed. *Down by the Riverside: Readings in African American Religion.* New York: New York University Press, 2000. Yet another competent collection of essays written by many of the leaders in the field of African American religious history. These essays are of uneven quality, but together they present a helpful, comprehensive picture of African American religion.

Murphy, Larry, J. Gordon Melton, and Gary L. Ward, eds. *Encyclopedia of African American Religions.* New York: Garland, 1993. The best single-volume reference work on African American religion.

The North Star: A Journal of African-American Religious History. http://northstar.vassar.edu. The leading scholarly journal devoted exclusively to the study of African American religious history.

Raboteau, Albert J. *Canaan Land: A Religious History of African Americans.* New York: Oxford University Press, 2001. An excellent, brief introduction to African American religious history. Not as comprehensive as *The Black Church in the African American Experience* (above) but just as competent and easier to read.

———. *Slave Religion: The "Invisible Institution" in the Antebellum South.* New York: Oxford University Press, 1978. A classic study of the religion of American slaves. This is still the best book on the invisible institution.

Sobel, Mechal. *Trabelin' On: The Slave Journey to an Afro-Baptist Faith*. Princeton: Princeton University Press, 1988. A detailed study of the rise of the black Baptist churches from the cultures of West Africa and American evangelicalism.

Wilmore, Gayraud S. *Black Religion and Black Radicalism: An Interpretation of the Religious History of African Americans*. 3rd ed. Maryknoll, NY: Orbis, 1998. An updated version of a classic study on religion and the black struggle for freedom and justice in America.

6

In Search of a Higher Christian Life

The Holiness, Pentecostal, and Charismatic Movements

And afterward, I will pour out my Spirit on all people. Your sons and daughters will prophesy, your old men will dream dreams, your young men will see visions. Even on my servants, both men and women, I will pour out my Spirit in those days. I will show wonders in the heavens and on the earth, blood and fire and billows of smoke. The sun will be turned to darkness and the moon to blood before the coming of the great and dreadful day of the LORD. And everyone who calls on the name of the LORD will be saved.

Joel 2:28–32

The Holiness-Pentecostal traditions usually receive short shrift in standard treatments of evangelicals. Their working-class roots and populist fruits have proven distasteful to learned elites.

Their heavy stress on radical holiness has unsettled conventional Christians. Moreover, their full-blown supernaturalism and effervescent worship often give pause to more restrained and critically minded evangelicals.

Yet the vast majority of evangelicals around the world today hail from Holiness, Pentecostal, and charismatic congregations—as do most in America's National Association of Evangelicals (NAE). In fact, Holiness, Pentecostal, and charismatic Christians comprise the fastest-growing population in the church.[1] They are devoted missionaries, international in their outlook, far more diverse than most Christian groups, and concerned to promote the gifts of both the clergy and the laity, men and women, rich and poor, young and old, regardless of status. They are new on the Christian scene, at least by most historical measures, but they have already started to make a deep impression on the church. Soon people from all walks of life, even those who walk the privileged corridors of worldly power, will pay attention—and not only when wayward TV preachers titillate the public with hypocritical financial and sexual escapades![2]

The chapter that follows traces the history of these radical evangelicals from their beginnings in the nineteenth-century Protestant mainline to their more recent exponential growth in the mainline and beyond.[3] Along the way, it suggests that though they dwell on the margins of media consciousness—and evangelical leadership—they represent a culmination of the evangelical quest for ever higher spiritual ground, for more intense and fervent commitment to reformation and renewal.

Called unto Holiness

In one sense, Holiness-Pentecostal concerns are as old as the church itself. It is not surprising, then, that Pentecostal leaders often date their movement to the pouring out of the Spirit at Pentecost (Acts 2). In another sense, however, America's Holiness, Pentecostal, and charismatic traditions enjoy a uniquely modern social, cultural, and intellectual history, one in which apostolic commitments to genuine holiness and the exercise of supernatural gifts have been reclaimed and used to spread the gospel abroad.

Beginning in roughly the 1830s, Christians in several denominations sounded an alarm about the domestication of evangelicalism, an alarm that eventually helped to gather the modern Holiness movement. As evangelicals inched to the center of the Protestant mainline, many felt they began to compromise their founders' intention to "be more vile" (in Wesley's words) for the sake of multicultural outreach. They had grown too fat and happy, claimed the more rigorous in their midst, far too comfortable with success at the top of America's "righteous empire." They showed troubling signs of selling out to secular moral values. They needed revival once again to reignite their passion for holiness.

This message resonated most clearly within America's Methodist Church, where it would echo Wesley's doctrine of "perfect love." The early Methodists maintained a goal of entire sanctification, or Christian perfection, which they believed could be had by faith during a supernatural "second blessing" from God. After conversion, Wesley taught, God continues to work within us, putting to death the deeds of the flesh and consecrating our lives for him. However, there comes a point for many when, dissatisfied with incremental progress in the faith, they seek and receive a second work of uniquely supernatural grace that lifts them to a new level of evangelical piety. Now entirely sanctified, they no longer want to commit sin. Of course, there is always room for growth in their relationship with God. But those who receive the second blessing no longer break his law voluntarily. They become radically committed to lives of perfect love.

Wesley himself sought this second blessing eagerly during his life. Significantly, however, he never claimed to have attained it. Most do not enjoy this privilege, he taught, until they are ready to die (in preparation for heaven). But many do receive it, he argued, long before they die. In fact, Wesley claimed to know several hundred "perfect" Christians personally. More importantly, he contended that the ideal of Christian perfection was taught in the Bible (in passages such as Matt. 5:48) and was essential as an inspiration to holiness.

Whatever the theological merits of the doctrine of perfect love, it played a powerful role in nineteenth-century moral reform, particularly through the rise of the Anglo-American Holiness movement. Though preachers of holiness often focused on issues of *personal* purity—exhorting Christians to avoid the corruption that comes with "worldliness" (and thus to flee temptations such as alcohol, the theater, and gambling)—they also supported a broader, counter-cultural, *public* righteousness that radicalized the social agenda of the evangelical empire. Mainstream evangelical leaders grew cautious and conservative (culturally speaking) by the end of the Second Awakening (that is, once they had a great deal to conserve), but their Holiness counterparts hearkened them back to the early years of the movement, calling them to renew their apostolic commitment to lives of selfless gospel witness regardless of status or personal gain. True, their appeals for moral purity featured lists of dos and don'ts, but not infrequently, these lists included a ban on owning slaves, a firm commitment to poor relief, and even a costly opposition to standard methods of Christian stewardship (especially the renting of pews to fund the work of local churches, a practice that visibly favored the rich—who enjoyed the best seats in the house—and sometimes excluded the poor completely from corporate worship). They also resulted in the formation of several new denominations committed to fleshing out such holiness to an extent nearly impossible in the Protestant mainline.[4]

Wesley's followers had promoted perfect love since the eighteenth century. In the early nineteenth century, Methodists such as Rev. Timothy Merritt (1775–1845) published guides to Christian perfection that were followed by thousands.[5] But it was not until the later 1830s and 1840s—when a new generation of preachers such as Rev. James Caughey (1810–91) and Phoebe Palmer (1807–74) repackaged the doctrine for mass consumption here and abroad—that it ignited and fueled the engine of modern Holiness.

Phoebe Palmer proved the most important Wesleyan-Holiness speaker. Born in New York, the fourth of fifteen children of Dorothea Wade Worrall and Henry Worrall (an Englishman who encountered Wesley personally), Phoebe grew up in the thick of Wesleyan Methodist culture. When only nineteen, she married a Rutgers-trained physician, Walter C. Palmer, and settled down in a house of her own in New York City. She gave birth to six children, only three of whom survived (eight of her own siblings died in childhood as well). She suffered a nearly fatal illness and then miraculously recovered. She joined the

Phoebe Palmer.
Courtesy of the Billy
Graham Center Museum,
Wheaton, IL.

Allen Street Methodist Church and witnessed a major revival
there (beginning in 1831). Her sister, Sarah Worrall Lankford
(1806–96), who also lived in New York City, underwent the second blessing and began to lead a series of prayer meetings for
local women in 1835. The following year, the Lankfords and the
Palmers decided to share a house in New York, at 54 Rivington
Street, a short walk from their church. Sarah and Phoebe began
their famous Tuesday Meeting for the Promotion of Holiness,
featuring Bible study, prayer, and inspiring spiritual testimonies,
especially those that pertained to sanctification. Phoebe received
the second blessing on what she called her "Day of Days" (July
26, 1837), laying her heart on the altar of devotion to her Lord.
The Tuesday Meeting took off, attracting hordes to the sisters'
home—at times hundreds would attend, and the meeting would
have to be moved—and inspiring similar meetings elsewhere

in the United States and overseas (in places as remote as India and New Zealand).

During the more than three decades that Palmer led the Tuesday Meeting, crowds of influential people flocked to hear her, including many pastors and bishops within her own denomination. The meeting began for women only but soon accommodated men. Palmer never sought ordination, but she outstripped the fame of most men with similar evangelical ministries, becoming a highly sought-after speaker at revivals and camp meetings (she spoke at over three hundred) as well as at colleges, divinity schools, and numerous other venues in the United States, England, Scotland, Wales, Ireland, and Canada. Her best-selling book, *The Way of Holiness* (1843), enhanced her reputation. She served as New York's first official, female Methodist "class leader" (i.e., formally appointed cell group leader). In short, she became her era's best-known evangelical woman and one of her era's best-known public figures.

Palmer taught listeners *not to wait* to experience entire sanctification. Most Wesleyans in her day endured a long period of prayer and earnest struggle for perfect love. Palmer invited people to count themselves dead to sin *immediately,* to trust the promises of God regarding entire sanctification, and to offer their lives—by faith—on the altar of the Lord (this teaching was known as her "altar theology"). Based on a rare interpretation of a cluster of Scripture texts (especially Matt. 23:19 and Heb. 13:10), she argued that Christ is both the sacrifice that atones for the sin of the world and the altar on which sinners can offer themselves before the Father. Moreover, not only is it possible to offer oneself on this altar, but it is the duty of every Christian to consecrate his or her life. As Palmer wrote in a typical passage on the promise of perfection:

> On everyone who will specifically present himself upon the altar . . . for the sole object of being ceaselessly consumed, body and soul in the self-sacrificing service of God, He will cause the fire to descend. And . . . He will not delay to do this for every waiting soul, for He standeth waiting, and the moment the offerer presents the sacrifice, the hallowing, consuming touch will be given.

138

One may ask, "How soon may I expect to arrive at this state of perfection?"

> Just so soon as you come believingly, and make the required sacrifice. . . . When the Saviour said, "It is finished!" then this full salvation was wrought out for you. All that remains is for you to come complying with the conditions and claim it. . . . It is already yours. If you do not now receive it, the delay will not be on the part of God, but wholly with yourself.[6]

At roughly the same time that Palmer developed her altar theology, Charles Finney charted a parallel version of can-do sanctification among America's Congregationalists and Presbyterians. As an aggressive moral reformer, Finney had long exhibited tendencies toward Christian perfectionism, but after he moved to Oberlin College, he took the time to systematize his understanding of sanctification. Along with Oberlin's first president, Rev. Asa Mahan (1799–1889), Finney crafted a peculiarly Reformed variation on the theme of perfect love known ever since by the name of Oberlin Perfectionism. He based it not on the Wesleyan doctrine of a momentous second blessing but, significantly, on Edwards's understanding of natural ability. Clearly, Oberlin Perfectionism put Finney at odds with an overwhelming majority of the Reformed (who usually *denied* that people can attain perfection this side of heaven), but it also helped non-Wesleyans to join the Holiness movement, guaranteeing it a pervasive role in evangelicalism.

The cardinal difference between the Oberlin and the Wesleyan views of perfection had to do with Finney's denial of the need for a second blessing. Working out of a more Reformed, gradualist model of sanctification, Finney paved the way for millions of non-Wesleyan evangelicals to consecrate themselves by means of an "overcoming life," or a "higher Christian life," a life devoted to the continual mortification of their sin.[7] Like Palmer, Finney called his listeners to *immediate* perfection. The pennant that flew above his revival tent read "Holiness unto the Lord," and the hot pursuit of sanctification proved a central theme in his preaching. But rather than plead with anxious auditors to claim the second blessing, he told them they had the natural ability to comply with God's commands—that is, to repent without delay and to obey God's will without exception.

Holiness themes suffused the nation during the antebellum period, but the interdenominational Holiness movement did not coalesce until just after the Civil War (1861–65), at first within the context of the camp meeting. Revivalism had continued to thrive long after the Second Awakening in camp meetings and numerous other venues across the country. A major businessmen's revival broke in 1857, pulling hundreds of thousands of people into urban prayer meetings. Massive revivals also filled the camps of Civil War soldiers—North and South—beginning in 1862. Personal holiness was emphasized at these and other events, but not until 1867, at a camp in southern New Jersey, was a revival held that focused first and foremost on this theme. It boasted ten thousand campers, most of them evangelical Christians. More importantly, it led to the institutional development of the modern, international Holiness movement.

On July 17, 1867, outside the town of Vineland, New Jersey, a group of holiness advocates calling themselves the National Camp Meeting Association for the Promotion of Holiness sponsored this ten-day-long revival on the theme of sanctification. Led by Rev. William B. Osborn (1832–1902) of the New Jersey Methodist Conference and Rev. John S. Inskip (1816–84) of the Green Street Methodist Church (in New York City), this first-ever Holiness camp meeting proved to be a rousing success. At its conclusion, the National Camp Meeting Association elected Inskip president and decided to sponsor a series of other Holiness camp meetings. Riding a wave of spiritual passion for the doctrine of sanctification, its leaders attracted more than twenty thousand to each of their next two meetings—first in Manheim, Pennsylvania (1868), then in Round Lake, New York (1869). Soon they founded a publishing house, started a Holiness periodical (the *Christian Witness and Advocate of Bible Holiness*, published from 1870 to 1959), formed a missions organization, and changed their name to the more inclusive National Holiness Association (later the Christian Holiness Association).

In the 1870s, especially, the Holiness movement went international. Phoebe Palmer and Charles Finney had preached revival tours through Britain in the 1840s, 1850s, and 1860s. Beginning in 1873, however, Robert Pearsall Smith (1827–99) and his wife,

Hannah Whitall Smith (1832–1911), exported explicitly Holiness doctrine and practice to Britain and beyond. Having received the second blessing themselves in 1867 (at the Holiness camp in Vineland), the Smiths commenced an extensive campaign of Holiness preaching, teaching, and writing throughout America, Great Britain, and the European Continent. Hannah became more famous than Robert—in part because Robert's ministry spiraled downward in 1875 when he was accused of counseling a woman in her hotel room unaccompanied. But Hannah's superior fame had much to do with her writing career as well. Her best-selling book, smartly titled *The Christian's Secret of a Happy Life,* appeared in 1875, after which thousands of people attended whenever she spoke about this theme. The Smiths' ministry culminated in 1875, at the Brighton (England) Convention for the Promotion of Christian Holiness. More than eight thousand people enrolled, primarily pastors and theologians, returning home so animated in support of scriptural holiness that a permanent, annual Holiness meeting was founded the following year. Known as the Keswick Convention, it continues to this day.

The Keswick Convention took its name from its location in Keswick, England, amid the idyllic Lake District made famous by England's romantic poets William Wordsworth (1770–1850) and Samuel T. Coleridge (1772–1834). It had precursors in other meetings that featured discussions of personal holiness, such as those at Mildmay Park (London) led by the evangelical Anglican priest Rev. William Pennefather (1816–73). But Keswick was the first devoted mainly to Holiness teaching. It tended to favor Reformed evangelicals, to muffle the doctrinal differences among Keswick participants, to prohibit perfectionist language, and to attract the leisure classes. It thus proved notably more conservative than some of its antecedents. But Keswick's winsome witness to what it called "victorious Christian living," or controlling the sinful nature by means of strenuous spirituality, rendered Holiness more popular than ever.[8] By the early twentieth century, upwards of ten thousand people gathered in Keswick every summer, and many leading American preachers imported Keswick themes back home.

Indeed, by the turn of the nineteenth century—largely due to Keswick's success at making Holiness teaching palatable to a broader range of tastes—the Holiness movement gained acceptance in the evangelical mainstream. A growing number of people, whether or not they affirmed perfectionism, responded to the call for uninhibited sanctification. Missions leaders such as A. T. Pierson, A. J. Gordon, and John R. Mott now stressed the link between entire consecration unto the Lord and the fulfillment of the Lord's Great Commission. Dwight L. Moody, in particular, plugged Keswick back in the States. Having visited Keswick during his famous preaching tours of England, Moody advanced its Holiness teachings during the 1880s and 1890s at his popular Northfield Conference (held every summer near his boyhood farm in Northfield, Massachusetts), where tens of thousands of people were trained in biblical knowledge and holy living and then exhorted to devote themselves to missions. In short, the Holiness movement was now sanctioned by all sorts of evangelicals and was heralded far and wide. Despite its growing popularity, however, not everyone in the movement swam in the mainstream.

The Rise of Pentecostalism

The most radical Holiness adherents still dwelt on the fringes of evangelicalism, both culturally and doctrinally. Most of them lived in the rural South, in small towns throughout the Midwest, or in working-class, urban neighborhoods. They tended to favor a strongly Wesleyan view of sanctification. As sophisticated versions of Holiness moved to the mainstream, these plebeians were left behind. More often than not, they did not know it. When they did, they usually chalked it up to common American worldliness and middle-class conformity.

By the end of the nineteenth century, most of these radical Holiness people had also left their former churches (usually the mainline Methodist Church) and had joined new, expressly Holiness spiritual bodies. Both the Wesleyan Methodist Church (1843) as well as the Free Methodist Church (1860)—now identifying formally as Holiness institutions—began to attract a new clientele. Additional Holiness churches were founded such as the Church of God, Anderson (1881), the Church of the Nazarene (c. 1895), and smaller black Holiness bodies such as the nearly

Charles Fox Parham.

Used by permission of the Flower Pentecostal Heritage Center.

forgotten Zion Union Apostolic Church (1869).[9] Many Holiness adherents convened outside formal church structures. In sum, radical Holiness people, sick and tired of mainstream apathy and longing for the restoration of apostolic faith, determined once and for all, as they said, to "come out from them and be separate" (2 Cor. 6:17). Significantly, it was from these new groups that modern Pentecostalism arose.

Though Pentecostal practices predate the twentieth century, the place to begin recounting the story of the Pentecostal movement is with the ministry of Charles Fox Parham (1873–1929).[10] In 1895, Parham left the Methodist Church and began to itinerate as an independent evangelist. He preached sanctification as a second work of grace. More importantly, he soon began to float the possibility of a potent "third blessing," a baptism *in* or *with* the Spirit[11] that would result in the soul's complete "infilling" by the Holy Spirit and a higher and more vibrant spiritual life than ever before. Parham had not (yet) received this blessing, but he believed it was attainable. He spent the rest of his life encouraging people to pursue it, providing a doctrinal point of reference for the Pentecostal movement.

Like many Holiness leaders, Parham practiced faith healing. In fact, in 1898, he took his ministry to Topeka and founded the Beth-el Healing Home, welcoming people seeking divine cures to stay and receive prayer. He engaged in outreach to the homeless. He founded a Holiness periodical (*The Apostolic Faith*). Most importantly, however, he started the Bethel Bible School (1900) in an opulent mansion in Topeka ("Stone's folly," so named because it impoverished the man who tried to build it), where he attracted thirty-four students for Bible study and Holiness training. Parham anticipated the outpouring of the Holy Spirit's power in a tremendous, global revival that would precede the return of Christ. He taught his students to expect it and to associate it with the promised baptism in the Spirit. The Bethel community soon anticipated a mighty and miraculous work of God.

By December of 1900, Parham concluded that what he called the "Bible evidence" that one had received the baptism in the Spirit was the gift of tongues.[12] He said this gift was part of the "latter rain" foretold in the book of Joel to be released in preparation for the final day of the Lord. Its recipients would be sent abroad to witness to the gospel—instantaneous missionaries who needed no language training at all—much as the first apostles did on the Day of Pentecost: "Tongues of fire" descended upon them, they "were filled with the Holy Spirit," and, miraculously, the foreigners in Jerusalem heard "them declaring the wonders of God in [their] own tongues" (Acts 2:3–4, 11). Soon the earth would be full of the knowledge of God as the waters cover the sea, and the Lord would return to earth in glory and would inaugurate the millennium. Needless to say, Parham's teaching aroused excitement in Topeka!

On New Year's Day 1901, one of Parham's students at Bethel, Agnes Ozman (1870–1937),[13] started to write in an unknown language (Chinese, as it was thought). Soon she was speaking in tongues as well. So were half of the others at Bethel. Revival ensued. Parham became a sensation virtually overnight. Before he knew it, several thousand people had flocked to his ministry. He preached another major revival toward the end of

1903, this time in small-town Galena, Kansas, near the state's southeastern corner. In early 1905, Parham moved to Houston, Texas, where he preached and planted churches in its rapidly growing suburbs.[14]

In December of 1905, Parham opened another Bible school, where he offered a ten-week training course in Pentecostal doctrine. Among the students he drew to Houston was an unassuming, thirty-five-year-old son of former slaves, a humble waiter turned Holiness preacher named William Seymour (discussed in chap. 5). Seymour was blind in one eye. He was a poor public speaker. Because he was black and segregation ruled the day in Texas, he had to sit outside the classroom near the door, carefully left ajar by Parham. However, despite his disadvantages and prejudicial treatment, Seymour quickly became convinced of Parham's Pentecostal teaching and went on to surpass his teacher in Pentecostal leadership. No one ever would have guessed it, but less than a year after Seymour enrolled in Parham's training course, he became the world's most famous Pentecostal ever![15] He soaked up everything he could before he left the school in Houston. Then in early 1906, he headed West to serve a fledgling Holiness mission in California, the Santa Fe Holiness Mission, named for its address on Santa Fe Street in Los Angeles.

On his first Sunday morning, Seymour preached on Acts 2:4, contending for tongues as Bible evidence of the baptism in the Spirit. When he returned to preach that night, he found the doors to the church padlocked. (Apparently, Pentecost would not be welcome soon on Santa Fe Street!) Seymour left with some of the members, holding services in the home of a man named Edward S. Lee, an African American Holiness layman more receptive to his teaching. Then he moved to the house of a Baptist couple on Bonnie Brae Street, where, on April 9, 1906, glossolalia broke out. Seymour and several other worshipers began to speak in tongues. Word of this spread like wildfire, eliciting so much interest that Seymour frequently had to preach from the porch to throngs of people lining the street. One day, the porch collapsed, unable to bear the weight above. No one was hurt (a fact interpreted as a miracle by eyewitnesses), but Seymour had to move—again.

He found an old, abandoned warehouse, twenty-four hundred square feet in size, on Azusa Street, the former home of an African Methodist Church (now the First African Methodist Church of Los Angeles).[16] He held three services a day, every day, for over three years. Thousands received the third blessing. Indeed, the Azusa Street Revival proved to be so influential that insiders still refer to it as "the cradle of Pentecostalism." Holiness-Pentecostal leaders from every part of the country—and even other parts of the world—came to witness the affair, returning home to spread the news about the restoration of Pentecost. Rev. Gaston B. Cashwell (1862–1916) of the Pentecostal Holiness Church attended and became the "Apostle of Pentecost to the South." Rev. William H. Durham (1873–1912), who worked at Chicago's North Avenue Mission, left Azusa Street with the gift of tongues and a passion to set the Windy City ablaze with Pentecost. Of course, Charles H. Mason also journeyed to Azusa, returning home to lead the Church of God in Christ into the fullness of the Pentecostal movement.

As alluded to already, the Azusa Street Revival proved unusually interracial, as did much of radical Holiness-Pentecostalism. In *How Pentecost Came to Los Angeles*, Frank Bartleman (1871–1936), the Azusa Street Revival's first historian, noted famously, "The 'color line' was washed away in the blood."[17] White, black, and Hispanic people joined in the daily worship services, heightening the sense of apocalyptic expectation. Indeed, in the *Apostolic Faith*, Azusa's regular newsletter, Seymour himself established an interracial tone for the revival:

> Apostolic Faith doctrine means one accord, one soul, one heart. May God help every child of His to live in Jesus' prayer. "That they all may be one, as Thou Father, art in Me and I in Thee; that they all may be one in us; that the world may believe that Thou hast sent me" [John 17: 21]. Praise God! O how my heart cries out to God in these days that He would make every child of His see the necessity of living in the 17th chapter of John, that we may be one in the body of Christ, as Jesus has prayed.[18]

This prayer was said to have been confirmed by the Holy Spirit at Azusa: "This meeting has been a melting time. The people are all melted together by the power of the blood and the Holy Ghost. They are made one lump, one bread, all one body in

Christ Jesus. There is no Jew or Gentile, bond or free, in the Azusa Street Mission."[19]

Likewise, the early Pentecostal leadership was gender inclusive. From the age of Maria Woodworth-Etter (1844–1924)—a popular preacher and faith healer whose spacious eight-thousand-seat revival tent was frequently too small to accommodate the crowds she drew—to that of Aimee Semple McPherson (1890–1944)—the preacher, healer, songwriter, author, and national radio personality who was ordained by William Durham (among others) and went on to found the Angelus Temple (1923) and even her own denomination, which she named the International Church of the Foursquare Gospel (1927)—women proved to be a major presence in Pentecostalism. More often than not, their churches refused to ordain them as elders and senior pastors. Nevertheless, large numbers were licensed to preach and heal the sick. In 1913, for example, women comprised 12 percent of the licensed clergy in the Church of God (Cleveland, Tennessee). By 1918, 21 percent of the preachers in the Pentecostal Assemblies of God were women. In the earliest years of the International Church of the Foursquare Gospel, nearly 37 percent of its preachers were women. Some African American Pentecostal churches were even more open to women. Ida Robinson's (1891–1946) Mt. Sinai Holy Churches of America, Inc. (1924) permitted women to serve in any role. Rev. Robinson herself presided as the church's bishop. After receiving a call from God, as she said, to "come out on Mt. Sinai and loose the women," she ranked the gift of tongues and entire consecration unto the Lord above more formal qualifications for ordination in her church.

After the heyday of Azusa Street and the movement's rapid rise, even Pentecostalism began to institutionalize. Not surprisingly, its early inclusivity decreased and its radicality subsided as its leaders sought to channel its flow of molten spirituality and to organize its millions of new adherents. After World War II, especially, Pentecostals also began to seek acceptance in more centrist evangelical social networks as well as in other mainstream American cultural contexts. They worked to polish their rough edges, to minimize their singularity. Many even softened their stance on the necessity of tongues. The movement continued to expand, becoming the fastest-growing segment of the evangelical world, but during the century's second half, its avant garde moved overseas.

In the United States alone, Pentecostals founded hundreds of denominational bodies, sponsoring building projects, missions boards, schools, and publishing houses. As discussed in chapter 3, these were crucial to the task of carrying on the work of revival, but they also meant a cooling off of the movement's eschatological zeal to repristinate "the unity of the Spirit" (Eph. 4:3). The work of accumulating and then controlling ministry resources fostered a spirit of factionalism among its multiplying members, a spirit exported by the ranks of Pentecostal missionaries. Today, there are thousands of Pentecostal denominations around the world, a curious statistic for a movement whose founders heralded a golden age of sanctified, millennial harmony.[20]

The most powerful Pentecostal denomination in the world remains the multimillion-member Assemblies of God (AG).[21] Founded in Hot Springs, Arkansas, in early April 1914, the AG hung out its shingle first in the town of Findlay, Ohio, then in St. Louis (1915), and, finally, in Springfield, Missouri, beginning in 1918. Rev. Eudorus N. Bell (1866–1923), a former Southern Baptist pastor, served as founding general chairman (later general superintendent). Rev. J. Roswell Flower (1888–1970) served as secretary-treasurer, remaining a fixture in the AG for half a century. (Flower is famous for pioneering the weekly *Pentecostal Evangel,* still a thriving publication, and for his lengthy term as AG general secretary.) In less than a century, the AG has grown from a tiny convocation of like-minded Pentecostals to one of the largest, most dynamic evangelical institutions. Even the sexual and financial sins of AG televangelists Jim Bakker (1940–) and Jimmy Swaggart (1935–)—scandals that filled the tabloids and lit the TV screens of the 1980s—seem not to have dampened lay enthusiasm for other AG ministries.

One of the most important features of AG's early history was the approval of William Durham's understanding of sanctification. As mentioned above, most early Pentecostals held to a Wesleyan view of sanctification as the fruit of a momentous second blessing. But Durham argued for what he preferred to call "the finished work of Calvary." Repudiating the need for a *second* work of special grace (i.e., subsequent to conversion)—or even the goal of instantaneous consecration unto the Lord—Durham claimed that Christ's atoning work ("the finished work of Calvary") is available at conversion and appropriated over the course of an "overcoming life." This more Reformed approach to growth in grace proved rather controversial, but Durham's mobility and persuasiveness as a Pentecostal preacher guaranteed it a bright future and opened the door to greater Reformed participation in the movement. Partly due, in fact, to its codification within the Assemblies of God, "finished work" has nearly won the day in Pentecostalism. Over the past one hundred years, whether Wesleyan or Reformed, most Pentecostals have *deemphasized* the doctrine of sanctification, stressing instead their *common* witness to the baptism in the Spirit and the higher Christian life that it empowers.

The Charismatic Movement

Though members of historically Pentecostal churches have done the salient work of explicating their commitment to the higher Christian life, charismatic leaders have popularized and marketed most Pentecostal practices to the Christian church at large. By definition, charismatics are those who have taken Pentecostalism into the mainline as well as into the realm of nonaligned congregations. Since the mid-twentieth century, they have done so with a passion. Consequently, every major Christian tradition in the world—in every sector of the globe—has now come under the sway of Pentecostalism.

Charismatics have been active promoting renewal around the globe since at least the 1940s (among black Anglicans in South Africa) and the 1950s (among evangelicals in Brazil). Some people claim that they were active in parts of Europe even earlier. In America, however, the charismatic movement did not command a great deal of attention until the spring of 1960, when Rev. Dennis Bennett (1917–91) and a group of his parishioners at St. Mark's Episcopal Church in middle-class Van Nuys, California, announced that they had spoken in tongues, received the baptism in the Spirit, and were meeting together for prayer and spiritual growth. Both *Time* and *Newsweek* covered the story. A major controversy ensued, dividing the churches of Los Angeles. Bennett's superiors forced him out to a smaller parish in Seattle.

But within a short time, every mainline Protestant body in the country had a contingent involved in charismatic renewal. In 1967, a major charismatic revival rocked the Roman Catholic Church at events spearheaded by the students of Duquesne and Notre Dame.

The movement mushroomed—so quickly, in fact, that its growth is nearly impossible to summarize well. Demos Shakarian (1913–93), a wealthy California dairy farmer, worked to organize the burgeoning ranks of charismatic laymen. His Full Gospel Business Men's Fellowship International (1951), founded to foster Pentecostal piety in ordinary laymen within a safe, ecumenical environment, soon was functioning as a hub for the whirling charismatic movement. One of the fellowship's supporters, Rev. Granville "Oral" Roberts (1918–), left the Pentecostal Holiness Church in 1968 to join the United Methodist Church, taking Pentecostal practices (such as faith healing and speaking in tongues) deep into the mainline. Rev. David du Plessis (1905–87), widely known as "Mr. Pentecost," had moved to the United States from South Africa in 1948. Remaining rooted in the historic Pentecostal denominations (first the Church of God, Cleveland, then the Assemblies of God as well), he befriended the charismatics, proving extremely ecumenical—stirring a hornet's nest of controversy with narrower Pentecostals—and became the twentieth century's leading Pentecostal spokesman to the global Christian community. Pat Robertson (1930–), ordained a Southern Baptist clergyman (1961), ran the Christian Broadcasting Network (CBN) beginning as early as 1959, turned it into one of the nation's leading television stations, entered the living rooms of millions of Americans each week, and gave unprecedented exposure to the concerns of charismatics. A major celebrity by the time he ran for president as a Republican in 1988, he won the Iowa caucuses, surprising all but his supporters. He ran out of steam in South Carolina and had to withdraw his candidacy. Moreover, his leadership of the religious right politicized the movement. But he did more than any charismatic in the world to promote the Pentecostal message in the nation's public square.

Since the early 1980s, charismatics have sidled closer to the center of evangelicalism, mainly through the independent congregational networks of the Calvary Chapel movement (1965) and the Vineyard Christian Fellowship (1982; 1985).[22] Rev. Chuck Smith (1927–), who was ordained by the International Church of the Foursquare Gospel, moved to Calvary Chapel, Costa Mesa, in 1965 (an independent congregation), preaching to twenty-five people near the California coast. Reaching out to hippies and surfers, he soon discovered himself at the center of the "Jesus People" movement, and, by the mid-1970s, he was shepherding nearly nine hundred conversions every month. He founded a series of Christian communes, a Christian music company (Maranatha Music), a multimedia ministry, and a cluster of Christian schools. He also spawned a host of other Calvary Chapel congregations, all mildly charismatic and completely evangelical. Today, there are hundreds of Calvary Chapel congregations around the world, and Smith's church in Costa Mesa serves roughly twenty-five thousand people.

Smith's most famous protégé, Rev. John Wimber (1934–97), got his start as a jazz and pop musician, having formed the Righteous Brothers group in 1962. Converted in 1963, Wimber became a fervent evangelist and Bible study leader. Then in 1971, he joined the staff of the Yorba Linda (California) Friends Church, which later became the Yorba Linda Calvary Chapel. He led the department of church growth at the fledgling Fuller Institute (1974–78) and later taught a controversial course at Fuller Seminary ("The Miraculous and Church Growth," 1982–85). He began to perform faith healings as early as 1977 and to advocate the appropriation of Pentecostal gifts. Then in 1982, he split with Smith and Calvary Chapel, joining a fledgling group of churches called the Vineyard. Always a strong personality, Wimber became the Vineyard's leader, and in 1985, he incorporated today's Association of Vineyard Churches. Smith and Wimber remained collegial, but Wimber favored a freer use of special, supernatural gifts in worship and evangelism. The Vineyard, like Calvary Chapel, now boasts hundreds of congregations. Thousands more have been affected by its popular worship style.

In fact, due to the success of Calvary Chapel and the Vineyard (among other, similar groups),[23] Pentecostal worship practices have infiltrated the mainline. Wimber alone published scores of the popular "praise songs" now used in corporate worship on nearly every part of the globe. Moreover, his California-style charismatic liturgy—with its pop music, open collars, and come-

John Wimber.

Used by permission
of the Flower
Pentecostal
Heritage Center.

as-you-are informality—has effected a massive change in the way most of us "do church."

Of course, Pentecostals have contributed much else to evangelicalism. Charismatic worship represents a popularization, a moderation, even a gentrification of Pentecostal practice (though in suburban churches the difference between the two is increasingly negligible), but it also represents, especially to non-Pentecostals, the most tangible manifestation of the Pentecostal movement. "Worship wars" are nothing new. Charismatics were not the first to employ contemporary music in the worship of the church. In fact, America's evangelicals have *usually* been attracted more to pop and folk singing than to classical hymnody. But today's most common conflicts over worship forms and styles usually occur along the charismatic front.

In roughly a century and a half, America's Holiness, Pentecostal, and charismatic movements have grown from a band of brothers and sisters intent on renewing the Protestant mainline

152

into a worldwide, ecumenical phenomenon. Now found in every Christian tradition in every corner of the world, uniquely Pentecostal passion for apostolic authenticity, the supernatural gifts, and energetic spirituality has excited the Christian piety and practices of billions. Perhaps the fastest-growing movement that the church has ever seen, Holiness-Pentecostalism—as conveyed by charismatics—has given the one, holy, catholic, and apostolic church a facelift, rendering its features more evangelical in the process.

Suggestions for Further Reading

Blumhofer, Edith L. *Restoring the Faith: The Assemblies of God, Pentecostalism, and American Culture.* Urbana: University of Illinois Press, 1993. The definitive scholarly treatment of the world's most powerful Pentecostal group.

Burgess, Stanley M., and Eduard M. Van der Maas, eds. *The New International Dictionary of Pentecostal and Charismatic Movements.* Rev. ed. Grand Rapids: Zondervan, 2002. The single best reference work on the Pentecostal and charismatic traditions.

Dayton, Donald W. *Discovering an Evangelical Heritage.* Peabody, MA: Hendrickson, 1976. A personal recovery of some of the radical roots of recent evangelicalism, penned by an opponent of the evangelical right.

———. *The Theological Roots of Pentecostalism.* Metuchen, NJ: Scarecrow, 1987. The best book available on the theology of Holiness and the theological background of the Pentecostal movement.

Dieter, Melvin E. *The Holiness Revival of the Nineteenth Century.* 1980; reprint, Lanham, MD: Scarecrow, 1996. A solid narrative history of the early Holiness movement.

Goff, James R. *Fields White unto Harvest: Charles F. Parham and the Missionary Origins of Pentecostalism.* Fayetteville: University of Arkansas Press, 1988. The definitive book on the ministry of Parham.

Goff, James R., Jr., and Grant Wacker, eds. *Portraits of a Generation: Early Pentecostal Leaders.* Fayetteville: University of

Arkansas Press, 2002. A fascinating glimpse at the lives of some of Pentecostalism's little-known early leaders.

Hollenweger, Walter J. *Pentecostalism: Origins and Developments Worldwide*. Peabody, MA: Hendrickson, 1997. The most important book by the man best known for claiming that William Seymour, rather than Charles Fox Parham, is the rightful founder of Pentecostalism (a movement Hollenweger depicts as most essentially interracial and inclusive).

Jacobsen, Douglas. *Thinking in the Spirit: Theologies of the Early Pentecostal Movement*. Bloomington: Indiana University Press, 2004. An overdue payment of respect to—and historical analysis of—the theological writings of twelve important, first-generation Pentecostals.

Jones, Charles Edwin. *Perfectionist Persuasion: The Holiness Movement and American Methodism, 1867–1936*. Metuchen, NJ: Scarecrow, 1974. A classic treatment of Holiness history in the Wesleyan traditions.

Oden, Thomas C. *Phoebe Palmer: Selected Writings*. New York: Paulist Press, 1988. The best place to start on Palmer's views and their significance.

Sanders, Cheryl. *Saints in Exile: The Holiness-Pentecostal Experience in African American Religion and Culture*. New York: Oxford University Press, 1996. The single best book on African American Pentecostalism.

Smith, Timothy L. *Revivalism and Social Reform in Mid-Nineteenth-Century America*. New York: Abingdon, 1957. A classic, paradigmatic treatment of the relationship between Wesleyan-Holiness views of sanctification and nineteenth-century evangelical social reform.

Synan, Vinson. *The Holiness-Pentecostal Tradition: Charismatic Movements in the Twentieth Century*. 1971; reprint, Grand Rapids: Eerdmans, 1997. The best introductory textbook on the Pentecostal movement.

Wacker, Grant. *Heaven Below: Early Pentecostals and American Culture*. Cambridge: Harvard University Press, 2001. A great read on the lived experience of early Pentecostal adherents. Written by one of the leading historians of American religion.

7

Standing on the Promises through Howling Storms of Doubt

Fundamentalism and Neoevangelicalism

Do not conform any longer to the pattern of this world, but be transformed by the renewing of your mind. Then you will be able to test and approve what God's will is—his good, pleasing and perfect will.

Romans 12:2

Unlike Pentecostals, who have suffered neglect in evangelical histories, fundamentalists and their so-called neoevangelical[1] heirs are often portrayed as both the alpha and the omega of the movement. There are many reasons for this. Their proximity to America's leading cultural institutions has attracted the attention of many outside evangelicalism. Their tendency to foster intellectual engagement has yielded a disproportionate

155

number of people writing on evangelicals who come from one or more of their educational institutions. Further, their leadership of flagship evangelical organizations often figures prominently within contemporary accounts of evangelical affairs, whether produced by evangelicals or not.

But as we have seen, evangelicalism is *not* fundamentalism and/or *neo*evangelicalism. Rather, the evangelical movement dates from the early eighteenth century—preceding the rise of fundamentalism by almost two hundred years. All of *today's* evangelicals have been touched by fundamentalism, but not to the same extent. Nor have they all responded alike. Many abandoned mainline Protestantism long before the period of its fundamentalist conflict. Many others proved more interested in issues of Christian piety than in the doctrinal matters dear to fundamentalist thinkers.

In the end, everyone smarted from the schisms that resulted from the fundamentalist controversy. The pages that follow, however, focus most intently on its evangelical *leaders*: those who stayed in the mainline until the early twentieth century, defending their faith—and seeking to keep control of the mainline Protestant churches—in an age beset by new mental and social challenges (fundamentalists); and those who regrouped after they lost the mainline Protestant institutions, building their own, mainly parachurch, web of evangelical ministries from which they would succeed in reengaging American culture (neoevangelicals).

Fundamentalists and their ilk are often depicted as reactionaries. This is not all wrong, for many did become reactionary after they lost the ability to swim with the big fish in the mainstream of mainline Protestant leadership and national cultural privilege. Some continue to react to liberal social trends without much cultural sensitivity or critical acumen. But in the early twentieth century, at the apex of the argument over naturalistic science and its bearing on the church (discussed below), fundamentalist leaders championed *steady* continuity with the tried and true traditions of Protestantism. In the late twentieth century, neoevangelicals appealed to cardinal verities of *historic* Christianity to revive the nation's spiritual inheritance, seeking a *restoration* of the religious values that governed the glory days of their righteous empire.

Indeed, fundamentalists and their neoevangelical progeny have stood steadfastly at the vanguard of the battle for the truth—the literal truth—of their beloved, everlasting gospel message. In the words of a popular hymn written in 1886 (by a disciple of D. L. Moody healed from heart disease by faith), "the promises of God" were not to be trifled with or qualified in the face of modern criticism. Christians were to trust in them, come hell or high water. They were to triumph, furthermore, by means of their calm, confident faithfulness to the Bible.

> Standing on the promises that cannot fail,
> When the howling storms of doubt and fear assail,
> By the living Word of God I shall prevail,
> Standing on the promises of God.[2]

The fundamentalists, and their neoevangelical descendants, have been known above all else for standing on the Word of God—and usually standing *under* it as well!

The Occasion of Fundamentalism

By the late nineteenth century, the intellectual ground had begun to shift under the feet of mainline Protestant officials, placing them closer than ever before to the forces of naturalism and modernism.[3] Doubt and even fear began to spread within the churches, as traditional, supernaturalistic views of God and the world gave way to modern, naturalistic criticism. Evangelicals, of course, had dealt with modern "infidelities" since the early days of their movement, but now the stakes were raised. For the first time ever, *accommodation* to such views, even to anti-Christian carping, had begun to carry the day among denominational activists. Some began to wonder about the future of Christianity. Fundamentalists resisted adaptation to these trends, bearing the brunt of the heaviest blows to Christian faith.

The two most devastating blows came from Darwinism and biblical higher criticism. Charles Darwin (1809–82) was not the first to promote a theory of evolution, but his use of natural history to elucidate its mechanism of natural selection[4] proved unusually impressive—both in its level of detail and by ren-

157

dering God superfluous to the evolution of species—sparking ideological firefights throughout the Western world. Further, the publication of his famous *Origin of Species* (1859) gained a surpassingly broad hearing for evolutionary thought. By the end of the nineteenth century, avant-garde theology teachers raced to appropriate his views (and those of other evolutionists), rejecting the historicity of Adam, Eve, the Garden of Eden, Noah's flood, the tower of Babel, and most of the rest of Genesis 1–11.[5] Popular preachers, such as Brooklyn's Congregationalist Lyman Abbot (1835–1922), published books promoting *The Evolution of Christianity* (1892), extolling *The Theology of an Evolutionist* (1897), and easing the way for widespread Christian acceptance of Darwinism.

German scholars did the most to develop the discipline of "higher"[6] critical study of the Bible—also known as historical criticism—the study, based primarily on extrabiblical sources, of the history *behind* the biblical texts. American scholars had engaged in it since the days of the Enlightenment. Even conservatives like Edwards and the founding theologians of the nation's seminaries endeavored to re-create the world of the biblical narratives. But in the late nineteenth century, largely due to the use of German models of secular education in America's leading colleges, biblical higher criticism began to *predominate* North American biblical studies. More significantly, the best higher critics now agreed that, for the sake of biblical science, they should treat the Bible "like any other book" (as their mantra went), ceasing to privilege the Bible's own accounts of its origins and authorship. Most maintained a *personal* faith in the God of Abraham, but a growing number set aside their doctrinal commitments to the teachings of the Bible—and its divine inspiration—in the name of more "objective" biblical scholarship.

The best-known scholar of the Bible in America at the time was Rev. Charles Briggs (1841–1913) of New York's Union Seminary. An ordained Presbyterian, Briggs pursued his graduate study at the University of Berlin (1866–69), immersing himself in the latest methods of higher criticism. After a stint in pastoral ministry, he joined the Union faculty and later earned a prestigious endowed chair in biblical studies (1891). In keeping with tradition, Briggs delivered a public lecture at his inauguration ceremony. He gave it a comforting title: "The Authority of Holy

Scripture." By the time he had finished speaking, however, most in the audience were squirming. Briggs denied that God inspired the very words of the biblical texts, that biblical teaching was inerrant, that biblical miracles had taken place by supernatural means, that biblical prophecy predicted the future with certainty and precision—not to mention several other Christian precepts. "I shall venture to affirm," he declared in a moment of provocation,

> that, so far as I can see, there are errors in the Scriptures that no one has been able to explain away; and the theory that they were not in the original text is sheer assumption, upon which no mind can rest with certainty. If such errors destroy the authority of the Bible, it is already destroyed for historians. Men cannot shut their eyes to truth and fact.[7]

Briggs did wind up affirming the inspiration and authority of the Bible's "essential contents," its "religion, faith, and morals," but lacking a stable set of criteria for determining what was "essential" in an admittedly errant Bible, he unloaded a heap of trouble on the Presbyterian Church.

Friends and colleagues rallied around him. Later that year, when some of his fellow Presbyterians tried him for heresy, Briggs received an acquittal from his New York Presbytery. Union supported him to the end. But conservatives in the churches raised a deafening hue and cry. Finally, the national Presbyterian General Assembly intervened, placing a veto on his appointment to the chair in biblical studies, suspending his pastoral credentials, and, at its meeting in Portland, Oregon, in 1892, endorsing biblical inerrancy and requiring its subscription on the part of future pastors (in a motion known ever since as the Portland Deliverance).

The Christian thinkers who did the most to counteract the forces of modernism were faculty members at Princeton Seminary. Founded in 1812, Princeton Seminary loomed as a rock of orthodoxy for years, refusing to budge in response to liberal criticism. In fact, its nineteenth-century stalwart, the polymath teacher, writer, and Presbyterian pastor Charles Hodge (1797–1878), boasted on more than one occasion, "I am not afraid to say that a new idea never originated in this seminary." Hodge did not intend to suggest that Princeton lacked in creativity but only that it favored a classical style of education. Princeton men were traditionalists. They believed that the *best* theology had already been produced and that their calling was to hand it down to future generations.

Hodge's son, A. A. Hodge (1823–86), along with his colleague B. B. Warfield (1851–1921), had formulated the seminary's stand on the doctrine of Scripture in a benchmark essay, "Inspiration," published first in the *Presbyterian Review* (1881). Inasmuch as it came to represent the stance of most conservative Protestants, especially in response to the claims of biblical higher critics, its most important paragraph is repeated below:

> It must be remembered that it is not claimed that the Scriptures, any more than their authors, are omniscient. The information they convey is in the form of human thought, and limited on all sides. They were not designed to teach philosophy, science, or human history as such. They were not designed to furnish an infallible system of speculative theology. They are written in human languages, whose words, inflection, constructions, and idioms bear everywhere indelible traces of human error. The record itself furnishes evidence that the writers were in large measure dependent for their knowledge upon sources and methods in themselves fallible, and that their personal knowledge and judgments were in many matters hesitating and defective, or even wrong. Nevertheless, the historical faith of the Church has always been that all the affirmations of Scripture of all kinds, whether of spiritual doctrine or duty, or of physical or historical fact, or of psychological or philosophical principle, are without any error when the *ipsissima verba* [very words] of the original autographs are ascertained and interpreted in their natural and intended sense. There is a vast difference between exactness of statement, which includes an exhaustive rendering of details, an absolute literalness, which the Scriptures never profess, and accuracy, on the other hand, which secures a correct statement of facts or principles intended to be affirmed. It is this accuracy, and this alone, as distinct from exactness, which the Church doctrine maintains of every affirmation in the original text of Scripture without exception. Every statement accurately corresponds to truth just as far forth as affirmed.[8]

The Bible, in other words, is clearly a human composition. All its pages bear the marks of humanity. But Scripture is also divine. Its very words were inspired.[9] Therefore, its *teachings*, although obviously expressed in finite forms, remain infallible, inerrant, and entirely true today. For old Princeton (as for many other conservative Protestants), God chose to relate to us in the flesh, in our own words, in water, bread, wine, and a host of other material manifestations. Those who want to know him well must thank him for such condescension, trust his methods, and cling to him humbly in these limited, earthly ways. Only in heaven will we see him face to face.

By the early twentieth century, most at Princeton favored biblical higher criticism and even made room in their theology for theistic evolution (i.e., evolution designed and superintended by God). But as late as 1874, Charles Hodge was claiming that Darwinism was "tantamount to atheism."[10] Even into the twentieth century, scholars such as Warfield—and his colleague J. Gresham Machen—upheld the utter truthfulness of Holy Scripture.

In our own day, when most *evangelical* scientists support a form of theistic evolution and most *evangelical* Bible scholars practice higher criticism, it may be difficult to imagine the fears of those who bucked these trends. It is important to remember, though, that most of the early backers of progressive accommodation also left behind the goal of doctrinal orthodoxy. Their "New Theology" not only sanctioned natural selection and secular biblical scholarship but also heralded human goodness over inherited depravity, a nebulous notion of "imminence" (God's presence and development, or "becoming," in the world) that subdued divine transcendence, and God's love to the neglect of his awesome holiness and wrath. In the words of H. Richard Niebuhr (1894–1962), who had been reared in this theology and harbored little affection for his fundamentalist peers, it taught "a God without wrath [who] brought men without sin into a kingdom without judgment through the ministrations of a Christ without a cross."[11]

In addition to the blows received from intellectual trends, evangelicals in this era were disoriented by their nation's massive social changes, especially the rapid growth of America's cities. In 1790, shortly after the nation's independence from England, only 5.1 percent of its citizens lived in urban areas. In 1870, 25.7

161

percent did. By 1920, 51.4 percent, more than half its people, dwelled in major cities. Another way of depicting the growth of America's urban landscapes is to say that in the years from 1800 to 1890 the nation's general population grew by twelvefold, while its urban population grew by eighty-seven-fold—more than seven times as fast as the nation at large! Chicago, for example, which had been a tiny hamlet only half a century earlier, was the fifth largest city in the world by 1890.

In response to urban growth, progressive Protestant reformers such as Washington Gladden (1836–1918) in Columbus, Ohio, and Walter Rauschenbusch (1861–1918) in New York promoted what later came to be called the social gospel. Their work was rooted in a critique of evangelical revivals—for their allegedly excessive concern with the souls of individuals and their ignorance of larger, more organic, social problems. But the social gospel arose with nineteenth-century socialism as well as the birth of sociology as an academic discipline that emphasized analysis of modern social structures. It sought to apply gospel principles to the practice of urban ministry, especially to the needs of the urban poor. By the late nineteenth century, it had inspired hundreds of pastors and other urban social workers to establish settlement houses and charter "institutional churches," congregations offering a wide range of social ministries—including bathing facilities, job training, and educational services—to America's working class. Liberal pastors such as Gladden published programmatic guides called *Social Salvation* (1902) and *The Church and Modern Life* (1908). Others such as Rauschenbusch wrote books on *The Social Principles of Jesus* (1916) and, most famously of all, *A Theology for the Social Gospel* (1917). Building on and also secularizing the fervent moral optimism that characterized the work of the righteous empire, some suggested that their effort to Christianize the social order would inaugurate a great millennial age, a golden age of the Holy Spirit defined not by revival but by the rule of social justice.

Evangelicals fretted about the social gospel's secularity. They worried that social gospelers were substituting social work for evangelism. Therefore, evangelical ministry leaders—notably D. L. Moody, J. Wilbur Chapman (1859–1918), Billy Sunday (1862–1935), and Moody Church's pastor Paul Rader (1879–1938), not to mention the black and Pentecostal leaders discussed

162

above—mounted their own urban campaigns, holding *revivals* for the common man on America's city streets. They also continued to show concern for the physical needs of "the least of these." In fact, evangelicals founded several hundred soup kitchens, or rescue missions, prior to 1900, ladling soup, soap, and salvation to the nation's down-and-outers. But their efforts usually focused on the individual sinner, placing the gospel message first and frequently forcing people to listen to an evangelistic sermon before receiving physical care. As in the case of slave missions, so with ministry to the poor, the goal of getting people to heaven trumped their needs in the here and now.

Critics of evangelicalism frequently exaggerate this aspect of its outreach, embroidering the line between its urban ministries and those of the social gospel movement (some of whose leaders were evangelicals). Nevertheless, they are right to say that by the late nineteenth century, when faced by a whole new world of needy people and social issues, evangelicals retreated from the front lines of reform. Their fears of social gospel liberalism, combined with the cultural pessimism connected to the spread of dispensational views among them, contributed to what is known as a "great reversal" of their posture in society—particularly in its modern, urban settings—one that has haunted evangelicals ever since.

As this story *usually* goes, the *post*millennial hopes of many early evangelicals fanned the flames of social reform in the righteous empire.[12] Because they believed that moral effort could help to usher in the millennium, evangelicals labored diligently for the needy. By the end of the nineteenth century, however, things began to change for the worse. *Pre*millennial eschatology, especially dispensationalism,[13] began to win the hearts and minds of evangelical leaders. Soon, most stopped behaving as though the world could be perfected. Dispensationalism taught them that the world was getting worse and that it would keep getting worse until the Lord returned to *rescue* those who believed in him from the great tribulation—and eventual conflagration—yet to come. They lost their motive for social reform. They thought that the world was going to hell or, more precisely, that the world was literally turning into hell. They started to spend the bulk of their energy pulling people *out* of danger, throwing lifelines to the lost, one soul at a time. A classic sermon by D. L. Moody ("The Return of Our Lord," 1877) symbolizes this shift succinctly:

> Some people say, "I believe Christ will come on the other side of the millennium." Where do you get it? I can't find it. The word of God nowhere tells me to watch and wait for the coming of the millennium, but for the coming of the Lord. I don't find any place where God says the world is to grow better and better. . . . I find that the earth is to grow worse and worse, and that at length there is going to be a separation. "Two women grinding at a mill; one taken and the other left; two men in one bed, one taken and the other left." The Church is to be translated out of the world. . . . I look on this world as a wrecked vessel. God has given me a life-boat, and said to me, "Moody, save all you can." God will come in judgment and burn up this world, but the children of God don't belong to this world; they are in it, but not of it, like a ship in the water. This world is getting darker and darker; its ruin is coming nearer and nearer; if you have any friends on this wreck unsaved you had better lose no time in getting them off.[14]

As the story usually concludes, in the realm of social reform, evangelicals turned into ostriches. They stuck their heads in the sand, ignoring the new, secular implications of their gospel message. Social reform became the province of liberal Protestants and Catholics, for evangelicals had abdicated their civic responsibility.

This standard story is full of hyperbole. Some premillennialists *resisted* dispensationalism, a fact that is usually lost on mainline critics.[15] Furthermore, many dispensationalists showed more love to the poor than social gospel partisans (who sometimes talked a better game than they actually played). But clearly, many other evangelicals abandoned social ministry. The story of their turnabout contains a kernel of truth. As lamented by their own, neoevangelical children, in the long run, the great reversal hurt their gospel witness, giving observers reason to think that they had become so heavenly minded that they were of no earthly good. In the short run, moreover, it exacerbated the evangelicals' differences with modernists, hastening the tug-of-war for Protestant control usually dubbed the "fundamentalist controversy."

Institutional Battles: Contending for the Faith

Early in the second decade of the twentieth century, a massive ecumenical movement of conservatives converged on a common opposition to modernism (mental *and* social) and an acclamation of the "fundamental," or cardinal, doctrines of the faith. Sharing an evangelical pedigree, the members of this movement, soon to be called "fundamentalists," had stayed loyal to the mainline during its nineteenth-century splits, but now they had nearly had enough. They felt that Christian faith was at stake, and they refused to stand by and watch their churches apostatize.

Several lists of fundamental Christian doctrines were defended, but the most popular among them was "The Five Point Deliverance" of the northern Presbyterians (1910). Still reeling from the blows received from Briggs and other liberals, the Presbyterian General Assembly ruled that all who wanted to be ordained within their presbyteries had to own the substance of the revised Westminster Confession[16] *and* affirm five doctrines, *unrevised* though newly challenged by progressives: (1) the inspiration and inerrancy of the Bible, (2) the virgin birth of Christ, (3) the substitutionary atonement of Christ, (4) the bodily resurrection of Christ, and (5) the historicity of the biblical miracles.

At roughly the same time, A. C. Dixon (1854–1925), R. A. Torrey (1856–1928), and several other luminaries published twelve volumes of essays on the fundamental doctrines called *The Fundamentals: A Testimony to the Truth* (1910–15). Two wealthy Presbyterian oilmen, Lyman (1840–1923) and Milton (1838–1923) Stewart, bankrolled the bulky venture, mailing three million sets of the books to ministers and missionaries in all parts of the world. Their contributors included marquee public intellectuals such as Warfield, A. T. Pierson, James Orr (1844–1913), and Charles Erdman (1866–1960). They opposed all kinds of modernism, from biblical higher criticism to theological liberalism, from naturalism to Darwinism to democratic socialism. Building on the momentum of the northern Presbyterians, they rallied people from several Protestant traditions to a least-common-denominator flag of orthodoxy. Not surprisingly, *The Fundamentals* soon became a standard of "fundamentalism."

By 1920, the conservatives entrenched along the Protestant mainline were poised for battle in defense of the fundamentals. In fact, in 1919, battle readiness was signaled by the launching of the interdenominational World's Christian Fundamentals Association (WCFA). Led by Rev. William Bell Riley (1861–1947), famous pastor of the First Baptist Church in Minneapolis and head of the Northwestern Bible and Missionary Training School (now Northwestern College), the WCFA capped a series of prophecy conferences convened within the shadow of World War I. It gathered conservatives concerned about the future of the world as well as their churches' preparation for the apocalypse. It also reinforced the resolve of anxious evangelical leaders "to contend for the faith that was once for all entrusted to the saints" (Jude 3, a favorite fundamentalist verse).

Finally, in 1920, Rev. Curtis Lee Laws (1868–1946), a Baptist minister and editor of the weekly *Watchman-Examiner*, coined the word *fundamentalist*. Evangelicals now identified their mission in the mainline with defense of the fundamentals, and therefore, in an editorial published in his northern Baptist paper, Laws referred to them as "fundamentalists." Today, many of us employ this word for people we dislike. We associate it with bigotry and religious zealotry. But Laws himself was a fundamentalist. He deemed it a badge of honor, for as he defined them in his paper, fundamentalists are those "who still cling to the great fundamentals and who mean to do battle royal for the faith."[17]

During the early 1920s, "battle royal" bludgeoned nearly every mainline Protestant body. Few of them met with amputations (or ecclesiastical schisms), but most hemorrhaged profusely. Northern Baptists and Presbyterians suffered the worst casualties. Northern Baptist fundamentalists organized in 1920 at a conference held in Buffalo ("Fundamentals of Our Baptist Faith") on the eve of the annual meeting of the Northern Baptist Convention (NBC). Founding the National Federation of Fundamentalists of the Northern Baptists, they quickly simplified their name to the Fundamentalist Fellowship (1921). They pushed for checks on the spread of liberal teaching in northern Baptist schools, the formal adoption of the New Hampshire Confession of 1833 (a moderately Reformed Baptist statement), and controls on the views of northern Baptist missionaries.

But the persistence of historic, anticreedal Baptist sentiment and intramural bickering by fundamentalist leaders led to defeat on all three fronts. At the NBC meeting in Indianapolis in 1922, it was "resolved, that the Northern Baptist Convention affirm that the New Testament is an all-sufficient ground for faith and practice, and we need no other statement"[18] (such as the New Hampshire statement of faith). Later the NBC endorsed its schools and current missionaries. Further, in 1923, the right-wing Baptist Bible Union split from the Fundamentalist Fellowship—a "second-degree separation"[19] led by Canada's T. T. Shields (1873–1955). By the end of the 1920s, fundamentalists had clearly lost control of the NBC. Thus, in 1932, the Baptist Bible Union became a separate Baptist denomination, today's General Association of Regular Baptist Churches (GARB). Later, in 1947, the remnant Fundamentalist Fellowship became the Conservative Baptist Association of America (CBA), today's CBAmerica.

Fighting was even worse among the northern Presbyterians. In 1922, the Baptist Harry Emerson Fosdick (1878–1969), who was serving on the staff of New York's First Presbyterian Church, preached an inflammatory sermon titled "Shall the Fundamentalists Win?" In it, he criticized the fundamentalist view of the virgin birth, the inerrancy of Scripture, and the second coming of Christ. He called on Christians to be "tolerant" of dissent within their churches and to remain "open-minded" in response to modern learning. Presbyterians had been fighting for several decades by this time, but Fosdick's sermon threw down the gauntlet for the church's final battle over modernistic trends.

Rev. Clarence E. Macartney (1879–1957) picked it up. Senior pastor of Philadelphia's Arch Street Presbyterian Church, Macartney struck back in a sermon titled "Shall Unbelief Win?" calling on the Presbyterian Church to censure Fosdick. Fosdick's friends showed support for their beleaguered modernist, but when the Presbyterian Judicial Commission requested that he help his cause by *joining* them officially as a Presbyterian pastor, he declined—unwilling to bind himself to the Westminster Confession (or any other, for that matter). Significantly, that year the Presbyterian General Assembly passed the Auburn Affirmation (1924), a document signed by nearly thirteen hundred Presbyterian clergy that repudiated "The Five Point Deliverance" of 1910 (which had been reaffirmed in 1916 and 1923). The affirmation lowered the bar for Presbyterian ordination, but Fosdick's liberal Baptist scruples held him back from taking the leap. After Fosdick served five years in the pulpit at Park Avenue Baptist Church (1925–30), John D. Rockefeller Jr. (1874–1960), Fosdick's friend and biggest supporter, built him his own magnificent perch, christened the Riverside Church for its location overlooking the Hudson River in Manhattan.[20] Fosdick served there until his retirement in 1946. To this day, it remains the flagship church of American Protestant liberals.

Just as Fosdick was deciding to leave the Presbyterian Church, its fundamentalists began to lose ground and beat a retreat. Their about-face began in response to the Auburn Affirmation (a devastating loss), but it ended in defeat with the transformation of Princeton. Beginning in 1914, when Rev. J. Ross Stevenson (1866–1939) was elected Princeton's president, a change took place regarding the seminary's ethos. Though a conservative man himself, Stevenson thought his school should serve the *entire* Presbyterian Church. Thus, he welcomed all its members, including moderates and liberals. Some conservatives objected, and his faculty divided. Then in 1923, Professor Machen sounded the alarm with the publication of his classic *Christianity and Liberalism*. He charged, defiantly, "despite the liberal use of traditional phraseology modern liberalism not only is a different religion from Christianity but belongs in a totally different class of religions." Furthermore, "the liberal attempt at reconciling Christianity with modern science has really relinquished everything distinctive of Christianity."[21] Machen held no punches, for he believed that modern liberalism had nothing at all to do with historic Christianity. It stood beyond the pale. Only the orthodox preserved "the faith that was once for all entrusted." If Princeton hoped to remain an honest-to-goodness Christian school, it had to reverse its trend of liberal accommodation.

Stevenson worked aggressively to marginalize Machen. Then in 1929, he showed him the door. The Presbyterian General Assembly of that year granted Stevenson authority to reorganize the school's administrative flow chart, control its curriculum, and keep conservative faculty from power. The fundamentalists withdrew. They forged the Delaware and founded their own school in Philadelphia, naming it, indicatively, Westminster Seminary

Westminster Seminary staff, early 1930s. *Bottom left to right*: **Ned Stonehouse, Oswald Allis, J. Gresham Machen, Cornelius Van Til, Paul Woolley.** *Top left to right*: **Allan MacRae and John Murray.** Used by permission of the Rolfing Memorial Library.

(1929). Machen was suspended from the northern Presbyterian clergy roster for his role in founding the Independent Board in 1935 (see chap. 4), so he and his followers began the Presbyterian Church of America (1936), which would later change its name to the Orthodox Presbyterian Church (1939).[22] To this day, people distinguish between the old and the new Princeton, for as Machen once muttered in reference to B. B. Warfield's funeral, "old Princeton—a great institution it was—died when Dr. Warfield was carried out."[23]

Nothing symbolized the defeat of mainline Protestant fundamentalists like their "victory" at the Scopes trial in Dayton, Tennessee (1925). John T. Scopes (1901–70), a junior teacher at the local public high school, was solicited by the fledgling American Civil Liberties Union (ACLU, 1920) to test his state's new law against the teaching of evolution. Clarence Darrow (1857–1938), a celebrity lawyer (and obstreperous agnostic), was retained for his defense; the prosecution was led by William Jennings Bryan (1860–1925). A famous Presbyterian populist and fundamentalist spokesman, Bryan had served as a federal congressman, a presidential candidate (three times), and the secretary of state under President Woodrow Wilson. But he had not tried a case in court for twenty-eight years. Darrow made him look foolish. The papers made him look even worse. The Scopes case, in fact, turned into a raucous "Monkey Trial." A total of twenty-two telegraphers sent 168,000 words per day from Dayton's courtroom to media posts around the world. Dayton's local chamber of commerce, which had helped the ACLU to bring the trial to Dayton's doors, capitalized on its publicity. Peddlers hawked souvenirs. A regional Baptist fundamentalist pitched a tent and preached to the crowds. By the time the trial had ended, few cared, or even noticed, that Scopes had lost. Fined one hundred dollars for teaching evolution, he never paid the state a dime. His conviction was later overturned on a technicality. Bryan died soon after the trial, literally exhausted by the fiasco. Fundamentalists, who were always strongest in northern, urban areas, have been ridiculed ever since as country bumpkins.

"Cooperation without Compromise": The Neoevangelicals

During the 1930s and 1940s, fundamentalists licked their wounds. Some withdrew into a hostile state of Christian separatism, giving up on the larger culture and defining themselves in opposition to mainline Protestantism (they took their ball and went home). But many others got back up and reinvested in the culture, repairing their ministries and reaching out to others. In fact, fundamentalism *grew* throughout this period of recovery—and has continued to grow apace—though usually out of the range of vision of cultural connoisseurs. Fundamentalists lost their place at the helm of the mainline Protestant churches. They were sidelined at the nation's elite educational institutions. But they survived, and even thrived, within America's heartland, which had never embraced the modernists or cared much for elitists.

Those who worked the most assiduously to reengage culture eventually called themselves the *new* (or neo-) evangelicals[24]—both to signify their youthful passion for social and cultural relevance and to distance themselves from antisocial forms of

170

Carl F. H. Henry.
Used by permission of the
Rolfing Memorial Library.

fundamentalism. They sported a new style of fundamentalist performance, projecting less concern to master the Christian martial arts than to reverse the dire effects of the great reversal. Indeed, they sought to revisit the best of *pre*-reversal evangelicalism, retaining their orthodox Protestantism but reaching out again in the mode of its eighteenth-century twist. As confessed by their leading thinker, Rev. Carl F. H. Henry (1913–2003), in a penitential unburdening of what he granted was *The Uneasy Conscience of Modern Fundamentalism* (1947), "the great majority of Fundamentalist clergymen, during the past generation of world disintegration, became increasingly less vocal about social evils."[25] But Henry went on, declaring his movement's desire to rectify this problem: "The cries of suffering humanity today are many," he began.

> No evangelicalism which ignores the totality of man's condition dares respond in the name of Christianity. Though the modern crisis is not basically political, economic or social—fundamentally

171

it is religious—yet evangelicalism must be armed to declare the implications of its proposed religious solution for the politico-economic and sociological context for modern life.[26]

His book has served ever since as the movement's cultural manifesto.

Evangelicals such as Rev. J. Elwin Wright (1890–1973) and Rev. Harold John Ockenga (1905–85) scurried to build support for the movement during the 1930s, but its first major foray into American public life came through the National Association of Evangelicals (NAE). In 1941, Wright and Ockenga convened a meeting of like-minded leaders at Moody Bible Institute. They sought to plan a forum for proactive evangelicals who were united in support of a common witness. Their group was wooed by Carl McIntire (1906–2002), a Machen protégé and recent founder of the separatistic Bible Presbyterians (1939), who wanted them to join his American Council of Christian Churches (1941)—a combative, antiecumenical remnant from their past. But they persisted in their effort to build a more inclusive fellowship, embracing all who would sign a fundamentalist statement of faith. The following year, their dreams were realized in a banquet hall at the Hotel Coronado in St. Louis, as 150 delegates from all across the country met at their National Conference for United Action among Evangelicals. The delegates birthed the NAE, elected Ockenga their president, and appointed Wright to serve as executive secretary. During the several years that followed, the NAE grew exponentially. It wrote a constitution (1943) and a seven-point doctrinal statement of faith (1943), founded a national Office of Public Affairs (1943), opened a lobby for media ministry (1944, the National Religious Broadcasters), founded a missions agency (1945) and a humanitarian arm (1945, World Relief), and started several other well-supported ventures. Today, millions of individuals from hundreds of institutions support the NAE and its motto, "cooperation without compromise," making it by far the single largest clearinghouse for common outreach by America's evangelicals.

During the late 1940s, evangelicals reentered the larger theological world, primarily through the ministries of Fuller Seminary (1947) and the national Evangelical Theological Society (ETS, 1949). The ETS emerged from the faculty lounge at Gordon

Harold John Ockenga.
Used by permission of
the Rolfing Memorial
Library.

Divinity School (1889, today's Gordon-Conwell Theological Seminary), whose teachers sought a broader intellectual community. Drawing a wide array of scholars to its bare-bones doctrinal statement (featuring biblical inerrancy), it sponsored annual meetings and, in 1958, started a theological journal (now the *Journal of the Evangelical Theological Society*). It proved enormously successful, enlisted several thousand members, and raised demand from evangelicals for doctrinal direction. By the 1960s and 1970s, many schools stepped in to supply it—especially Gordon and its recently refurbished counterpart, Chicago's Trinity Evangelical Divinity School (TEDS, 1884).[27] But in the 1940s and 1950s, it was Fuller that led the way.

Rev. Charles E. Fuller (1887–1969), an orange-grower-turned-pastor and host of the popular radio show *The Old Fashioned Revival Hour,* enjoyed twenty million listeners worldwide. So when he determined to found "a Cal Tech of the evangelical world," he already owned a mass marketing tool for advertising

173

Charles E. Fuller.

Used by permission of the Rolfing Memorial Library.

the school. Christian radio was booming by the time of World War II, thanks to the pioneering efforts of Paul Rader, Aimee McPherson, and Percy Crawford (1902–60) of Youth for Christ. In fact, by 1948, just as Fuller opened his doors, over sixteen hundred evangelical programs aired per week. Mainline Protestants received "sustaining-time" air slots free of charge from stations all around the country. Evangelicals, however, had to pay for air time. Even so, they came to dominate the world of Christian radio, dwarfing most of the programs of their mainline counterparts. Indeed, when Fuller promoted his school over the nation's radio waves, he was guaranteed a crowd. When they arrived in Pasadena to start their theological studies, he guaranteed that they would receive a good education. Harold Ockenga served as Fuller's founding president, commuting from Boston before the days of frequent flyers (1947–54, 1960–63). His founding faculty included the best in fundamentalism: Everett

Harrison (1902–99) in Bible, Carl Henry in theology, Harold Lindsell (1913–98) in history and missions, and Wilbur Smith (1894–1976) in apologetics. For many years, they were the deans of neoevangelical thought.

Evangelicals have always been determined media mavens. Long before the invention of radio—not to mention television and the Internet—they worked as energetic scribes, saturating the world of print with the gospel message. Today, they fashion best-selling books from publicly traded publishing houses in locations such as Nashville and Grand Rapids. But during the 1950s and 1960s, at the height of the neoevangelical impact on America, their most important publication was *Christianity Today* (1956), a magazine first edited in Washington, D.C. (later in Carol Stream, Illinois). It was begun by Billy Graham and his father-in-law, L. Nelson Bell (1894–1973), a former missionary doctor (in China) and leading southern Presbyterian. As Graham remembered later of the magazine's inception, "I was awakened one night at about 2 A.M. I went to my desk and wrote out ideas about a magazine similar to the *Christian Century* [the leading mainline/liberal journal], one that would give theological respectability to evangelicals. . . . I thought the articles should appeal especially to men who were open to the biblical faith in the mainline denominations, but the magazine had to be thoroughly evangelical."[28] He later shared his vision with Bell. The two of them asked Wilbur Smith to serve as their founding editor. Smith declined, so Graham and Bell turned to Carl F. H. Henry, who had been recommended by yet another at Fuller, Harold Lindsell.

In their opening installment, Henry and company announced their mission: "Neglected, slighted, misrepresented—evangelical Christianity needs a clear voice, to speak with conviction and love, and to state its true position and its relevance to the world crisis."[29] They sought to infiltrate the culture with a winsome gospel witness, the kind of witness that had always impelled the evangelical movement. Graham himself was exceedingly winsome. Only thirty-eight years old by the time the magazine was founded, he had been a household name for several years. In 1949, at a revival in Los Angeles, he had been "puffed" (or publicized) within the papers of media mogul William Randolph Hearst (1863–1951), best known as the subject of a film

Billy Graham. Courtesy of the Billy Graham Center Archives, Wheaton, IL, and the Billy Graham Evangelistic Association, Charlotte, NC.

by Orson Welles, *Citizen Kane* (1941). Soon he was on the cover of *Time, Life,* and *Newsweek* magazines. Hundreds of thousands of admirers, even Hollywood celebrities, hurried to hear him preach. He took advantage of his fame to raise support for the magazine, and with the help of people like oil magnate J. Howard Pew (1882–1971), he and his board were able to donate complimentary subscriptions to nearly every Protestant minister in the country. Some of these two hundred thousand leaders were later dropped from circulation, and in 1967, this policy had to be abandoned. But during its crucial early years, *Christianity Today* was read for free by movers and shakers far and wide.

By the late 1950s, neoevangelical leaders had succeeded in their goal of reengaging American culture. Signs of success hung all around. Evangelicals had access once again to the levers of power. Their ministries were prospering. Their numbers were abounding. More Americans went to church than ever before.[30] Many now looked to these descendants of the fundamentalist controversy to lead the global evangelical movement. Not surprisingly, however, as the movement had expanded it had also diversified, exceeding the grasp of the neoevangelicals. Graham and his colleagues tried their best to keep their growing family together, but despite their recent success in reviving fundamentalism—and American culture at large—some of their siblings became uncomfortable with their leadership. A few conservatives, in fact, began to grow wary of Graham himself, going public with their fears beginning in 1957.

After Pope Pius XII (1939–58), Billy Graham was the most popular Christian figure in the world. He was the confidant of presidents. Millions had attended his evangelistic crusades. Millions more had read about them in the press. In 1957, he held a crusade in New York City, preaching to throngs in Times Square and Madison Square Garden. Some of the services were even aired on national television. So when his ushers seated mainline Protestant leaders on the platform, and Martin Luther King Jr. offered a prayer of invocation, the world was watching—and some of his erstwhile fundamentalist friends were fuming. This was the first time that Graham had welcomed nonevangelical sponsors to an American crusade,[31] some of whose churches would receive the converts counseled at his meetings. This was also three years after Graham had finally desegregated his southern events for good, a move that had stirred more than a few wasp nests in the land of Dixie.

Right-wing fundamentalist leaders, most of whom ministered in the South—Bob Jones Sr. (1883–1968), Bob Jones Jr. (1911–97), John R. Rice (1895–1980), and several others—now opposed Graham publicly, disparaging the *new* evangelical movement he led. They encouraged their constituents to turn their backs on Graham, creating a rift in the evangelical world. From that point forward, many ardent fundamentalists refused to share fellowship with backers of "cooperative revivalism," insisting on a strict, second-degree separation.[32] Graham's supporters, most of whom were never thrilled with fundamentalism and some of whom were not even raised in fundamentalist families, departed even further from the label "fundamentalist," identifying themselves simply as evangelicals.[33]

Ruffling feathers even further, neoevangelical leaders began to differ on doctrinal grounds. Fuller Seminary softened its stand on biblical inerrancy at a faculty/trustee planning conference in 1962. In 1970, it dropped the doctrine from its statement of faith, causing controversy that echoed all over the evangelical world. Harold Lindsell, by then the editor of *Christianity Today*, published an exposé of Fuller and its theological shift. Titled *Battle for the Bible* (1976), it championed biblical inerrancy, challenged evangelicals to doctrinal fidelity, and excoriated Fuller for its marked drift to the left.

Since that time, of course, evangelicals have diversified further, disagreeing over a host of social and theological questions. Should women seek ordination? Should congregations rock 'n' roll? How much do people need to know about the gospel to be saved? These and other contested issues still divide the movement deeply, leading some, as we have seen, to doubt the usefulness of the term *evangelical* altogether.

What is more, just as some are ready to leave the term behind, those who cherish it the most—latter-day neoevangelicals—have become more fully aware of just how far the evangelical world extends beyond their grasp, both at home *and* overseas. In the 1950s and 1960s, they could presume to lead this world. Whether or not everyone followed, their reputation (and resources) ensured the mobilization of a broad base of support. But today's evangelicals are much more independent and far more self-sufficient. Many despair over the likelihood of bringing evangelicals together, projecting a bear market for evangelical futures. Some analysts are calling for a major disinvestment. And the founding neoevangelical leaders are passing away. The question remains whether others will arise to take their place, finding a way to choreograph this massive, motley Christian movement without requiring its members (futilely) to march in single file.

Suggestions for Further Reading

Bendroth, Margaret Lamberts. *Fundamentalism and Gender, 1875 to the Present.* New Haven: Yale University Press, 1993. The best book available on fundamentalist women and the role of gender issues in the fundamentalist movement.

Carpenter, Joel. *Revive Us Again: The Reawakening of American Fundamentalism.* New York: Oxford University Press, 1997. The standard history of fundamentalists (and neoevangelicals) in their period of recovery—after they lost control of the mainline—roughly 1925 to 1950.

Graham, Billy. *Just as I Am: The Autobiography of Billy Graham.* San Francisco: HarperSanFrancisco, 1997. A good, easy read on the life and work of America's foremost twentieth-century evangelical.

Hangen, Tona J. *Redeeming the Dial: Radio, Religion, and Popular Culture in America.* Chapel Hill: University of North Carolina Press, 2002. The remarkable story of the rise of fundamentalist radio from its start in the 1920s through its flourishing at mid-century. Features the radio ministries of Paul Rader, Aimee Semple McPherson, and Charles Fuller.

Hart, D. G. *Defending the Faith: J. Gresham Machen and the Crisis of Conservative Protestantism in Modern America.* Baltimore: Johns Hopkins University Press, 1994. The most scholarly treatment of Machen and his role in fundamentalism.

Larson, Edward J. *Summer for the Gods: The Scopes Trial and America's Continuing Debate over Science and Religion.* Cambridge: Harvard University Press, 1998. A Pulitzer Prize–winning book on the Scopes "Monkey Trial."

Long, Kathryn. *The Revival of 1857–58: Interpreting an American Religious Awakening.* New York: Oxford University Press, 1998. The standard scholarly treatment of the businessmen's revival and its role in paving the way for fundamentalism.

Longfield, Bradley J. *The Presbyterian Controversy: Fundamentalists, Modernists, and Moderates.* New York: Oxford University Press, 1991. Offers a wealth of detail on the fundamentalist controversy in the Presbyterian Church in the U.S.A. (the northern Presbyterians). Focuses on the roles of six key Presbyterian leaders (spanning the ideological spectrum): J. Gresham Machen, William Jennings Bryan, Henry Sloane Coffin, Clarence Macartney, Charles Erdman, and Robert Speer.

Marsden, George M. *Fundamentalism and American Culture: The Shaping of Twentieth-Century Evangelicalism, 1870–1925.* New York: Oxford University Press, 1980. The best book ever written on the rise of fundamentalism.

179

————. *Reforming Fundamentalism: Fuller Seminary and the New Evangelicalism*. Grand Rapids: Eerdmans, 1991. An institutional history of Fuller that also offers what has become the standard view of the rise of neoevangelicalism.

Moberg, David O. *The Great Reversal: Evangelism versus Social Concern*. Philadelphia: J. B. Lippincott, 1972. The classic source on the great reversal.

Sandeen, Ernest R. *The Roots of Fundamentalism: British and American Millenarianism, 1800–1930*. Chicago: University of Chicago Press, 1970. Although outmoded by Marsden's books (above), Sandeen is best on the powerful role of premillennialism in shaping fundamentalism.

Smith, Christian. *American Evangelicalism: Embattled and Thriving*. Chicago: University of Chicago Press, 1998. An excellent book on recent evangelical social and cultural engagement. Written by a Christian sociologist, it demonstrates what Smith has called "the reversal of the great reversal."

Trollinger, William Vance. *God's Empire: William Bell Riley and Midwestern Fundamentalism*. Madison: University of Wisconsin Press, 1990. The definitive treatment of the Minneapolis pastor and educator who founded the World's Christian Fundamentals Association.[34]

Conclusion

The Future of Evangelicalism

Then I saw a Lamb, looking as if it had been slain, standing in the center of the throne. . . . He came and took the scroll from the right hand of him who sat on the throne. And when he had taken it, the four living creatures and the twenty-four elders fell down before the Lamb. Each one had a harp and they were holding golden bowls full of incense, which are the prayers of the saints. And they sang a new song: "You are worthy to take the scroll and to open its seals, because you were slain, and with your blood you purchased men for God from every tribe and language and people and nation. You have made them to be a kingdom and priests to serve our God, and they will reign on the earth."

Revelation 5:6–10

Centrifugal forces of various kinds continue to push at evangelicals, in America as much as anywhere else. Southern Baptists, for example, have been embroiled in civil war since well before 1979, when conservatives began to win control of their institutions. With a national membership approaching sixteen million people, they are still the largest Protestant church in the land. As long as their membership persists in this long-standing, family feud—and some of their people isolate themselves from other evangelicals—they will threaten the coherence of the evangelical movement.[1]

On a broader, national scale, a conglomerate of confessionalists has recently emerged to challenge evangelical pietism and pragmatism. They castigate our superficial lists of personal dos and don'ts as well as our anti-intellectual experientialism, calling us back to sixteenth-century forms of Protestant faith and practice—and questioning the legacy of our eighteenth-century twist. Led by Calvinists such as Michael Horton and D. G. Hart (see chap. 1), they also include confessional Lutherans in their institutional work, most notably, the Alliance of Confessing Evangelicals (ACE), syndicated radio shows such as *The White Horse Inn,* and publications such as Horton's *Modern Reformation* magazine and Hart's somewhat more earthy *Nicotine Theological Journal* (which he edits with John R. Muether).[2]

In a very different way, the charismatic movement continues to diversify our gene pool, filling it with a steady stream of colorful variations—from the laid-back "Jesus freaks" of sunny Southern California to Greek Orthodox believers in Ft. Wayne and Destin, Florida. A resurgent female leadership and women's ministries are now expanding the range of evangelical activism. (As discussed above, women have always comprised a majority of the evangelical movement, though their ministries have often been curtailed or controlled by men.) New immigration is also adding color to American evangelicalism, brightening it with faces from Latin America and Asia.

In fact, since the benchmark Immigration Act of 1965,[3] Hispanic[4] and Asian American[5] immigrants have quietly contributed several million new adherents to the evangelical movement. Anglo-American evangelicals are largely unaware of the massive scale of this development and have yet to offer much in the way of outreach to (or with) these brothers and sisters in the gospel (especially Hispanics, more of whom are working class). Nonetheless, theirs will likely be the next major chapter in the ongoing adventure of evangelicals in America, which has always been a multicultural nation of immigrants.

Of course, the *neo*evangelicals no longer have the capacity to unite our movement alone. The fact is, they never did. Nor did many of them want to. This does not, however, render solidarity a pipe dream. It simply means that we are past the days of defining ourselves primarily in opposition to others, namely, those deemed responsible for "mainline" degradation. Evangelicals lost the battle for control of the mainline, but we won, or at least are winning, the larger war for Protestantism. In fact, it might be said that we now comprise a new "mainline," one that is far larger and more diverse than the one we lost in the 1920s—and even the one we reengaged in the 1930s, 1940s, and 1950s.

Today, we face more global challenges, those of a privileged majority, not a dissident minority. Fresh leadership is required as well as a new, more global vision, a humbler spirit of partnership, and stronger support for the common good (especially the welfare of the poor). Guiding the movement will be difficult. Our leaders will have to unify a family larger than ever, one with a host of historical reasons to keep one another at arm's length. But if they take a look around them, they will discover a wealth of capital in evangelical history for getting the job done.

Evangelicals have always shared a strong centripetal faith, one that has held us together despite obvious differences. Ever since the Great Awakening, we have joined hands across all kinds of social and cultural obstacles, emboldened by the need to offer a common gospel witness and committed to the maintenance of historic Christianity. At times, our unity hinders us from honoring our differences; at other times, our differences can overwhelm our unity. But when we are at our best, we agree to disagree about a wide range of secondary and tertiary matters, not because they are unimportant or unworthy of expression in our *separate* institutions (I, for one, believe they are crucial) but because they are less important than our *corporate* Christian mission: to proclaim the gospel together, showing the world the love of God and doing everything we can to help the needy. Most of our national ministry leaders have embraced this mission firmly, from Calvinists such as Whitefield to Arminians such as Palmer, from Pentecostals such as Seymour to dispensationalists such as Moody. After nearly three centuries of working on this mission, we have learned a few lessons that can guide us into the future.

First, *the church needs evangelicals*. All too often, modern Protestants have forced people to choose *between* orthodoxy and ecumenical outreach. Either people choose a group that majors in theological purity, turns in on itself, and yields dry and withered fruit, or they join an ecumenical, socially active Christian organization that is unwilling to bind itself (when the going gets rough) to doctrines not pertaining directly to ecumenical work or justice. Evangelicals have often forced this kind of decision, usually erring on the side of doctrinal purity. But at our best, we have offered theological fidelity and ecumenical outreach simultaneously. This kind of comprehensive witness is essential to the fulfillment of Jesus' high priestly prayer with theological integrity (John 17).

Second, *at its best, evangelicalism functions as a renewal movement within the larger, universal church*. We have a tendency to be splitters, a trait that has aided our success in the modern economy of religion, which has always rewarded entrepreneurial target marketers. However, we also need to be joiners. Otherwise, we will lose our impact on the larger Christian church.

Evangelicals have usually been most faithful and prophetic when a minority within a larger group. Our cutting edge is often blunted by the kind of insularity—even arrogant self-sufficiency—that is bred by popularity (as it was in both the late-nineteenth and the late-twentieth century). Ever since the eighteenth century, some within our movement have pursued their own purity by separating themselves from the Christian church at large, siphoning resources from the groups left behind and letting the rest of the people of God suffer the consequences. Especially today, as evangelicals comprise a new majority, we need to be intentional about *serving* the rest of the church. We need to help one another resist the urge to go our own way, acting as Christian lone rangers and presuming that we are the be-all and end-all of the Holy Spirit's work around the world. Of course, with unreached people groups, we often have to go it alone. But in the main, we need to beware, lest we grow as high and mighty as the established churches we helped to undermine.

Finally, and relatedly, *evangelicalism is not enough*. We must stay rooted in the ground of Christian tradition. The eighteenth-century twist was a boon to Protestant faith and witness, but insofar as we have parted from the rest of the Christian church and the best of its resources, we have severed our own roots and starved our membership. Indeed, especially in this era of phenomenal success—when it is possible to live, from cradle to grave, within the confines of the evangelical movement—we simply must sink more and deeper roots in Christian history.

Too many of our leaders look no further than Edwards and Wesley, if indeed they look that far, for ministerial resources. But one of the reasons why these men remain such helpful models today is that their own Christian leadership was funded heavily by classical orthodoxy and early Protestantism. We must recall, as they did, that we evangelicals have never had a theology of our own. Precisely *because* we committed ourselves to multicultural partnership, we have always had to rally around a sparse doctrinal platform. We have always been dependent on much older Christian sources of doctrinal, especially ecclesiological, substance.

Nonetheless, as we have seen, evangelicals have changed the face of the world. Despite our sins and other shortcomings, God continues to use us in the building of his kingdom. Evangelicals, in fact, are presently bursting at the seams—so much so that we are finding it hard to keep ourselves together or to distinguish ourselves from some of the many cultures we have imbued.

In this postmodern age of self-fashioning, moreover, efforts at unifying people across their own in-group identities and divergent personal preferences come under strident criticism. Diversity, personal choice, and liberation are all the rage, even in many pockets of evangelicalism. This is certainly not all bad; in fact, much of it is good. Gospel people, above all, know the blessings of liberation and the multifarious makeup of the worldwide kingdom of God. But evangelicals also know the peril of worldly co-optation. Many wonder whether the world is now so much a part of us that our traditions of common witness may be lost in dissolution.

I pray that the burden of this book—to refresh our shared, historical memory—may help us to regain our spiritual bearings. And I trust that a fresh appropriation of our common heritage, though surely limited severely by our own historical blinders, can be used by God to bless the church for many years to come.

Notes

Preface

1. David B. Barrett and Todd M. Johnson publish an annual table detailing church demographics and world missions in every January issue of the *International Bulletin of Missionary Research*. At press time, the most recent table available was found in vol. 28 (January 2004): 24–25.

2. For helpful analysis of these trends, see Philip Jenkins, *The Next Christendom: The Coming of Global Christianity* (New York: Oxford University Press, 2002).

3. Throughout this book, I use the term *American* to refer to residents of the United States of America. My apologies to others living throughout the Americas (i.e., the Western Hemisphere) who object to such a usage. I follow it only for the sake of economical expression.

4. "Great Awakening" is a largely American term for the transatlantic revivals of the eighteenth century. British Christians usually refer to the revivals—collectively and more simply—as "the evangelical revival."

5. As noted on the copyright page, all Scripture quotations are from the New International Version (NIV). Most early evangelicals used the King James Bible, but the NIV has proved to be the most popular version in evangelical circles since its publication in 1973.

Chapter 1

1. *Christianity Today,* August 9, 1999, 62.

2. Alister McGrath, *Evangelicalism and the Future of Christianity* (Downers Grove, IL: InterVarsity, 1995), 55–56.

3. David W. Bebbington, *Evangelicalism in Modern Britain: A History from the 1730s to the 1980s* (London: Unwin Hyman, 1989), 2–3.

4. Most of these groups are discussed below. For the sake of clarity, however, a brief description of the differences between Calvinists and Arminians (which will be mentioned several times) may be in order. Calvinists are followers of the French Reformed pastor and theologian Jean Calvin (1509–64)—spelled in English, John Calvin—who emphasized the depravity of unconverted sinners and the sovereignty of God in choosing some (and not others) for salvation, regardless of merit. Arminians are followers of the Dutch theologian Jakob Hermans (1560–1609)—Jacob Arminius—who opposed Calvin's doctrine of divine predestination and emphasized the role that sinners play in their own conversions. The differences between Calvinists and Arminians came to a head at the Dutch Reformed Synod of Dordt (1618–19), from whose proceedings English Calvinists derived the famous "five points of Calvinism." Of course, there is far more to Calvinism than five simple points. Nonetheless, the five letters of the TULIP acronym (inspired by the floral passions of the Dutch Reformed) have summarized for many (not least the Arminian "remonstrants") the essential doctrinal tenets of the Calvinists: Total depravity (of unregenerate sinners); Unconditional election (of those redeemed by God from sin); Limited atonement (Christ's saving work on the cross atoned for only the sins of the elect); Irresistible grace (saving grace never fails to effect conversion); and Perseverance of the saints (once converted the elect will never fall from saving grace).

5. The best known of Webber's taxonomies is found in Robert E. Webber, *Common Roots: A Call to Evangelical Maturity* (Grand Rapids: Zondervan, 1978), 31–33. But see also Robert E. Webber, "Who Are the Evangelicals?" *USA Today* 115 (1987): 89.

6. Timothy L. Smith, "The Evangelical Kaleidoscope and the Call to Christian Unity," *Christian Scholar's Review* 15 (1986): 125–40.

7. Randall Balmer, *Mine Eyes Have Seen the Glory: A Journey into the Evangelical Subculture in America* (New York: Oxford University Press, 1989), 229–30.

8. Robert Johnston, "American Evangelicalism: An Extended Family," in *The Variety of American Evangelicalism*, ed. Donald Dayton and Robert Johnston, 252–72 (Knoxville: University of Tennessee Press, 1991).

9. Donald W. Dayton, "Some Doubts about the Usefulness of the Category 'Evangelical,'" in *Variety of American Evangelicalism*, 251. See also Donald W. Dayton, "The Holy Spirit and Christian Expansion in the Twentieth Century," *Missiology: An International Review* 16 (1988): 403; and idem, "'Evangelical': More Puzzling Than You Think," *Ecumenical People Programs Papers*, Occasional Paper no. 29 (May 1988): 5–6.

10. Michael Horton, "The Battle over the Label 'Evangelical,'" *Modern Reformation* 10, no. 2 (March/April 2001): 16; and D. G. Hart, *Deconstructing Evangelicalism: Conservative Protestantism in the Age of Billy Graham* (Grand Rapids: Baker Academic, 2004), 16.

11. Though the terms *orthodox* and *orthodoxy* are hotly contested today, they prove more accurate as descriptors of the evangelical movement than the term *conservative*. Evangelicals have always been doctrinally conservative, but they have not always been culturally or politically conservative.

Chapter 2

1. There were also many Lutherans in Hungary and Transylvania, a chaotic region during this period that was dominated by Roman Catholics and Ottoman Muslim occupiers. Further, significant minorities of Reformed were living in places such as France and the Polish-Lithuanian Commonwealth, often without the formal protection of their magistrates.

2. When assigning dates to individuals, I provide the years of the reigns of kings and queens and the years of birth and death of all others.

3. Others from Wesley's Holy Club helped with the revival, most notably Benjamin Ingham (1712–72), a powerful preacher who labored in Yorkshire and eventually joined the Moravians.

4. The Wesleys' friends Benjamin Ingham and Charles Delamotte (1714–86) accompanied them.

5. Elisabeth Jay, ed., *The Journal of John Wesley: A Selection* (Oxford: Oxford University Press, 1987), 15.

6. Ibid.

7. Ibid., 34–35.

8. Ibid., 41.

9. Ibid.

10. Quoted in Iain H. Murray, *Jonathan Edwards: A New Biography* (Carlisle, PA: Banner of Truth Trust, 1987), 163–64.

11. Ibid., 162.

12. Though Frelinghuysen was born in Germany, he ministered in New Jersey's Raritan Valley under the auspices of the Dutch Reformed Church.

13. Jonathan Edwards, *Letters and Personal Writings*, ed. George S. Clayhorn, *The Works of Jonathan Edwards*, vol. 16 (New Haven: Yale University Press, 1998), 792–93.

14. George Whitefield, *A Select Collection of Letters of the Late Reverend George Whitefield*, 3 vols. (London: Edward & Charles Dillz, 1772), 1:393–94.

Chapter 3

1. Historians estimate that one-third of the churches in Connecticut and one-fifth of the churches in Massachusetts experienced schism as a result of the Awakening.

2. In the colonial period of American history, colleges were populated primarily by teenage boys.

3. Richard L. Bushman, ed., *The Great Awakening: Documents on the Revival of Religion, 1740–1745* (New York: Atheneum, 1970), 51–53.

4. Though, technically speaking, there is nothing Arminian about this doctrine, some have cited it as a source of the popular evangelical adage that Christians should think like Calvinists but act like Arminians.

5. Jonathan Edwards, "The Reality of Conversion," in *The Sermons of Jonathan Edwards: A Reader*, ed. Wilson H. Kimnach, Kenneth P. Minkema, and Douglas A. Sweeney (New Haven: Yale University Press, 1999), 83, 92.

6. The term *Christendom* refers to the territory and the ideal of state-sponsored Christian nationalism, both of which date back to the conversion of the Roman Emperor Constantine (in AD 312), the establishment of Christianity by

Emperor Theodosius I as the *only* legal religion of the ancient Roman Empire (in AD 380), and the geopolitical agenda of the Holy Roman Empire (which emerged in AD 800, lasted in one form or another through the period treated here, and gave to Christendom its definitive, medieval shape).

7. In 1776, the U.S. population was 2.6 million. By 1860, it had grown to 31.5 million, representing a more than twelvefold rate of increase since the Revolution. Relatedly, in only the half century between 1790 and 1840, over four million people moved west of the Appalachian Mountains, a number larger than that of the entire population during the Revolution.

8. From 1780 to 1818, 35 percent of Methodist itinerants died between the ages of twenty-three and twenty-nine. Another 27 percent died between the ages of thirty and thirty-nine. For more information about the circuit riders, consult the works by Hatch and Wigger listed among the "Suggestions for Further Reading" at the end of this chapter.

9. The tradition of Methodist circuit riding continues to this day. Although the American frontier vanished at the end of the nineteenth century, Methodist bishops still discourage their preachers from settling down for long, moving them every few years to new locations. Powerful, tall-steeple preachers sometimes evade the call to move (with the help of devoted, wealthy parishioners), and many bishops have begun to apply this policy more flexibly. But for the most part, Methodist preachers are still *supposed* to think of themselves as ready servants of the church at large. The world is still their parish!

10. Charles G. Finney, *Revivals of Religion* (Old Tappan, NJ: Revell, n.d.), 15.

11. Ibid., 2–3.

12. Despite the controversy they caused, Finney's new measures survived the era of the Second Great Awakening and (as many readers will recognize) persist in various forms of evangelical worship today.

13. W. P. Strickland, ed., *Autobiography of Peter Cartwright, the Backwoods Preacher* (Salem, NH: Ayer Company, 1972), 48–49.

14. Philip Schaff, *Church and State in the United States, or the American Idea of Religious Liberty and Its Practical Effects*, Papers of the American Historical Association, vol. 2, no. 4 (New York: Putnam's Sons, 1888), 9.

Chapter 4

1. The *magisterial* Reformers were leaders like Luther (1483–1546), Zwingli (1484–1531), and Calvin (1509–64) who promoted the Reformation with the help of their civil *magistrates*, frequently by the power of the sword. They are distinguished in textbooks from the *radical* Reformers, commonly called the Anabaptists, many of whom were avowed pacifists and all of whom were sectarians who favored what we would call the separation of church and state (though at times they took up arms and tried in vain to establish independent municipalities).

2. The Jesuits, technically known as the Society of Jesus, are a Catholic monastic order founded in 1534 to promote reform within their church, oppose the Protestant Reformation, and engage in missions work around the world (especially work that relates to the spread of Catholic education). Since

1967, the Congregation for the Propagation of Faith has been referred to as the Congregation for the Evangelization of Peoples.

3. The term *Huguenots* refers to French Reformed Protestants. Its etymology is contested, but since the middle of the sixteenth century, it has connoted the persecution and frequent exile of this group from their heavily Catholic native land.

4. Gisbertus Voetius (the Latinized form of his name), *Selectae Disputationes Theologicae*, 5 vols. (1648–69); and *Politica Ecclesiastica*, 3 vols. (1663–76).

5. Solomon Stoddard, *An Answer to Some Cases of Conscience, Respecting the Country* (Boston: Green, 1722), 11–12.

6. Solomon Stoddard, *Whether God Is Not Angry for Doing So Little towards the Conversion of the Indians?* (Boston: Green, 1723), 6.

7. Robert Millar, *The History of the Propagation of Christianity and Overthrow of Paganism*, 2nd ed., 2 vols. (London: G. Strahan, 1726), 1:ix.

8. Ibid., 1:xiv.

9. Ibid., 1:xii, 2:592.

10. See Jonathan Edwards, *A Humble Attempt to Promote Explicit Agreement and Visible Union of God's People in Extraordinary Prayer for the Revival of Religion and the Advancement of Christ's Kingdom on Earth, Pursuant to Scripture-Promises and Prophecies Concerning the Last Time* (Boston, 1747). Available in Jonathan Edwards, *Apocalyptic Writings*, ed. Stephen J. Stein, *The Works of Jonathan Edwards*, vol. 5 (New Haven: Yale University Press, 1977), 307–436.

11. Jonathan Edwards, *The Life of David Brainerd*, ed. Norman Pettit, *The Works of Jonathan Edwards*, vol. 7 (New Haven: Yale University Press, 1985), 96.

12. William Carey is often referred to as the "father of modern missions," though as we have seen, this appellation does not quite fit.

13. Quoted in Dana L. Robert, *American Women in Mission: A Social History of Their Thought and Practice* (Macon, GA: Mercer University Press, 1996), 98.

14. By the end of the nineteenth century, the colonization movement had sent nearly sixteen thousand black Americans "back to Africa."

15. Designating such "firsts" is hard to do. In this case, the designation is complicated by the fact that Rev. David George (who is discussed in the next chapter) preceded Coker in Sierra Leone, as did the black Quaker businessman Paul Cuffe (1759–1817). Both were African colonizers, but neither is (usually) considered a foreign missionary.

16. Quoted in Robert, *American Women in Mission*, 96–97.

17. Ibid., 1.

18. Mrs. E. F. Chilton, "Woman's Work," *Woman's Missionary Advocate* 1 (July 1880): 13.

19. Tellingly, A. J. Gordon's full name was Adoniram Judson Gordon. A. T. Pierson was rebaptized in 1896, after which he was removed from the Presbyterian ministry.

20. Until recently, this hymn was published in most evangelical hymnals. See, for example, *Hymns for the Living Church* (Carol Stream, IL: Hope Publishing, 1974), 472.

21. Buck won the Pulitzer Prize in 1932 for *The Good Earth* (1931), a novel detailing the difficult life of Wang Lung, a peasant farmer. She won the Nobel

Prize for literature in 1938 after releasing several other books that dealt with the Chinese (and their interloping missionaries).

22. The Commission of Appraisal, William Ernest Hocking, chairman, *Rethinking Missions: A Laymen's Inquiry after One Hundred Years* (New York: Harper & Brothers, 1932), ix.

23. Ibid., 326, 65, 70.

24. Ibid., 61–62, 19.

25. The Aucas are known technically as the Huaorani. Many Huaorani accepted the gospel after the deaths of the Auca martyrs, whose story was told by Elliot's widow, Elisabeth Howard Elliot (1926–), most famously in two nationally acclaimed best-sellers: *Through Gates of Splendor* (New York: Harper, 1957); and *Shadow of the Almighty: The Life and Testament of Jim Elliot* (New York: Harper, 1958).

26. The "majority church" is a recent term that refers to the church in the non-Western world, where the majority of Christians live (see the preface for basic statistics).

27. Though the United States is no longer the world's largest sender of full-time, or career, missionaries, its number of short-term missionaries is rising rapidly. In fact, the best recent estimates suggest that American churches, Christian colleges, and missions agencies are sending more than one million short-term missionaries each year. Many thanks to Robert Priest for information on short-term missions.

28. The "10/40 window" is a recent term referring to a long rectangular window, or geographical belt, that stretches across the length of North Africa and much of Central Asia (from 10 degrees to 40 degrees north of the equator), where most of the world's unreached people groups reside.

Chapter 5

1. Peter Randolph, "Plantation Churches: Visible and Invisible," in *Afro-American Religious History: A Documentary Witness*, ed. Milton C. Sernett (Durham: Duke University Press, 1985), 64.

2. Quoted in Alan Gallay, "Planters and Slaves in the Great Awakening," in *Masters of Slaves in the House of the Lord: Race and Religion in the American South, 1740–1870*, ed. John B. Boles (Lexington: University Press of Kentucky, 1988), 33.

3. Quoted in Philip D. Morgan, *Slave Counterpoint: Black Culture in the Eighteenth-Century Chesapeake and Low Country* (Chapel Hill: University of North Carolina Press, 1998), 427.

4. Quoted in Edward J. Blum, "Gilded Crosses: Postbellum Revivalism and the Reforging of American Nationalism," *Journal of Presbyterian History* 79 (2001): 290.

5. Martin Luther King Jr., "Letter from Birmingham Jail, April 16, 1963," in *Afro-American Religious History*, 437.

6. George Whitefield, *Three Letters from the Reverend Mr. G. Whitefield* (Philadelphia: B. Franklin, 1740), letter 3.

7. Frederick Douglass, "Slaveholding Religion and the Christianity of Christ," in *Afro-American Religious History*, 100–109.

8. Randolph, "Plantation Churches," 67.

9. Ibid., 67–68.

10. Quoted in Thomas Wentworth Higginson, "Slave Songs and Spirituals," in *Afro-American Religious History*, 113–14.

11. Ibid., 112.

12. Joseph H. Jackson, "National Baptist Philosophy of Civil Rights," in *Afro-American Religious History*, 428.

13. Accurate denominational membership statistics are notoriously difficult to maintain, but at the beginning of the twenty-first century, the historic black denominations reported the following membership totals: National Baptist Convention, U.S.A., Inc., 8 million (a controverted figure); National Baptist Convention of America, 3.5 million; Progressive National Baptist Convention, Inc., 2.5 million; African Methodist Episcopal Church, 2 million; African Methodist Episcopal Zion Church, 1.2 million; Christian Methodist Episcopal Church, 886,000; Church of God in Christ, 5.49 million. At press time, the African Methodist Episcopal Zion Church and the Christian Methodist Episcopal Church were working toward but had not yet completed a formal merger.

14. Richard Allen, "Life Experience and Gospel Labors," in *Afro-American Religious History*, 142.

15. Jon Butler, *Awash in a Sea of Faith: Christianizing the American People* (Cambridge: Harvard University Press, 1990), 129–63.

Chapter 6

1. Though the theological boundaries between Holiness, Pentecostal, and charismatic Christianity are often blurry, a few simple definitions may prove helpful at the outset. Holiness people are evangelicals with an unusually strong commitment to living a higher Christian life—that is, a more holy life, one set apart from worldliness and devoted to supernaturally empowered spirituality. Pentecostalism is rooted in the concerns of the Holiness movement but also includes a more fervent commitment to the special gifts of the Spirit (the supernatural gifts depicted in the biblical book of Acts and treated at greatest length by Paul in 1 Corinthians 12–14)—most distinctively, the gift of speaking in tongues (glossolalia). Charismatics have imported the goods of both groups back into the so-called mainline denominations and, more recently, into newer, independent congregations and networks of congregations (often called "neo-charismatic"). Chronologically speaking, the North American Holiness movement arose within the Protestant mainline during the early nineteenth century; Pentecostalism began in newly separated groups of Holiness adherents at the end of the nineteenth century; charismatics rose to prominence toward the middle of the twentieth century. Throughout this chapter, I use the lowercase form of "holiness" when referring in a generic way to the subject of Christian holiness; I capitalize the word when referring in a special way to aspects of the Holiness movement proper.

2. In recent years, Pentecostals themselves have entered the corridors of power, as attested most visibly by the appointment of Pentecostal John Ashcroft as America's attorney general (in 2001).

3. As discussed throughout this book, the cultural authority and the membership of the mainline denominations changed dramatically over the course of the

nineteenth century—and changed yet more dramatically during the twentieth century. New denominations proliferated in the wake of disestablishment (and have done so ever since); Holiness-Pentecostal, African American, and, later, fundamentalist groups broke out and formed their own churches beginning after the Civil War; and a host of non-Christian religions spread throughout the United States during the late twentieth century. As a result, the so-called mainline was decentered in America. A series of ecumenical mergers has helped to prop up its membership totals (which have otherwise fallen steadily since about the 1960s). But mainline churches—such as the post-Puritan United Church of Christ, the Episcopal Church, the Presbyterian Church (U.S.A.), the Methodist Episcopal Church, the Christian Church/Disciples of Christ, and, most recently, the Evangelical Lutheran Church in America—no longer represent the mainstream, driving force, or cutting edge of American Christianity. Some now suggest, in fact, that we should call these groups the "oldline."

4. The best-known among them were the Wesleyan Methodist Church (1843), founded by ardent abolitionists, and the Free Methodist Church (1860), which favored free pews, the freedom of slaves, and freedom of worship. After the institutionalization of an interdenominational, transatlantic Holiness movement (see below), other denominations formed along explicitly Holiness lines—such as the Church of God (Anderson, Indiana, 1881), the Church of the Nazarene (c. 1895), and the Salvation Army (which began in the slums of London, England, in 1865, but "opened fire" on the United States in 1880).

5. Merritt's best-known publications were *The Christian's Manual: A Treatise on Christian Perfection, with Directions for Obtaining That State* (1825) and the well-worn Holiness periodical, *The Guide to Christian Perfection*, which he edited from 1839 to 1945 (later renamed the *Guide to Holiness* and controlled by Phoebe Palmer).

6. Quoted in Melvin E. Dieter, *The Holiness Revival of the Nineteenth Century*, 2nd ed. (Lanham, MD: Scarecrow Press, 1996), 24.

7. This more "Reformed" approach to holiness would be symbolized for many in *The Higher Christian Life* (1858), a popular book by the Presbyterian minister William E. Boardman (1810–86), whose title soon became a catchphrase in the broader Holiness movement. Boardman moved his home to England late in 1875, where he became an important figure in British Holiness as well.

8. This theme was codified in a book by Keswick speaker Evan H. Hopkins (1837–1919), *The Law of Liberty in the Spiritual Life* (1884), which remains in print today.

9. As estimated by Vinson Synan (see bibliography below), nearly two dozen Holiness sects emerged in the South alone between 1893 and 1900 (when roughly one hundred thousand Holiness people left the Methodist Church).

10. Pentecostal origins are vigorously contested. While most specialists place them near the work of Parham, some insist that William Seymour (discussed again below) is the movement's true founder. Still others argue for the priority of Rev. B. H. Irwin (b. 1854), who founded the Iowa Fire Baptized Holiness Association in 1895 and, after a revival the following year in western North Carolina at which it is claimed that people spoke in other tongues, played an important role in shaping early Pentecostal practice. Little documentation sur-

vives to support the claims for Irwin's priority. Nonetheless, he is also said to have been the first to promote the Pentecostal doctrine of Spirit baptism (discussed below). In recent years, scholars have shown that Pentecostal phenomena (such as tongues speech and faith healing) occurred on every continent in the world (except Antarctica!) before the rise of Pentecostalism. Indeed, Pentecostal gifts have been around since the days of Pentecost. Still, they did not proliferate, contributing to the rise of a major Pentecostal movement, before the activity sparked by Irwin, Parham, and Seymour.

11. These prepositions are important. Parham and later Pentecostals distinguished between baptism *in* or *with* the Holy Spirit (often referred to as Spirit baptism) and baptism *of* the Holy Spirit (which is received at regeneration). In earliest Pentecostal thought, then, there were three special, supernatural blessings given to seekers: the (first) blessing of regeneration (the baptism of the Holy Spirit); the (second) blessing of Christian perfection (or entire sanctification); and the (third) blessing, complete infilling (baptism in the Spirit), which was accompanied by the gift of speaking in tongues. Holiness groups that refused to join the Pentecostal movement (such as the Church of the Nazarene) affirmed the first two blessings but repudiated the third.

12. Parham is widely regarded today as the inventor of the doctrine of tongues speech (glossolalia) as the sine qua non of baptism in the Spirit. However, for Parham, tongues speech was always for spreading the gospel abroad. It was "xenoglossia," technically speaking, the ability to communicate in a real, foreign language—a doctrine discarded by most as the movement grew and people learned that the tongues they spoke were not preexisting languages (at least not usually).

13. Ozman would later marry and take the last name of LaBerge.

14. At about this time (1903–5), in New Quay, Wales (on Cardigan Bay), a major revival occurred that helped to inspire a host of Pentecostals. There were reports of glossolalia, as some were said to have spoken in what was considered a dead Welsh tongue. The revival also involved a number of other Pentecostal practices and included several who went on to serve as Pentecostal leaders. Led primarily by Evan Roberts (1878–1947), a miner and blacksmith turned evangelist, it was boosted in America by the account of S. B. Shaw (b. 1854) titled *The Great Revival in Wales* (1905).

15. Parham's racist views, his rigid insistence on xenoglossia as the only true glossolalia, and the persistent rumors that he had engaged in homosexual practices (he was arrested on charges of sodomy in San Antonio, Texas, during the summer of 1907) kept him from playing a major role in the spread of Pentecostalism.

16. Sadly, this building has since been razed—initially to make way for a parking lot in what is now "Little Tokyo" in Los Angeles. Its lot is now the site of a plaza next to a Japanese American cultural center.

17. Frank Bartleman, *How Pentecost Came to Los Angeles: As It Was in the Beginning*, in *Witness to Pentecost: The Life of Frank Bartleman*, ed. Donald W. Dayton (New York: Garland, 1985), 54.

18. William J. Seymour, "The Baptist of the Holy Ghost," *Apostolic Faith* (May 1908): 3. My thanks to Joseph L. Thomas, a doctoral candidate at Trinity, for material from the *Apostolic Faith*. For more information on Pentecostal inter-

racialism, see Thomas's forthcoming dissertation, "'No Jew or Gentile': The Rise of Interracial Fellowship in Early Holiness-Pentecostalism."

19. Anon., *Apostolic Faith* (December 1906): 1.

20. The denominations below represent the most influential Pentecostal groups in America. Sorted by doctrinal orientation, they are listed in the order of their founding. (Some were started as Holiness churches and only later labeled themselves Pentecostal.) (1) Wesleyan (in terms of their view of sanctification): Pentecostal Holiness Church, Inc. (1895; 1975); Church of God, Cleveland (1886); Church of God in Christ (1897); and Church of God in Christ, International (1969). (2) Reformed (i.e., non-Wesleyan): Assemblies of God (1914); Pentecostal Church of God (1919); and International Church of the Foursquare Gospel (1923; 1927). (3) "Oneness" (i.e., nontrinitarian): Pentecostal Assemblies of the World (1907); Apostolic Overcoming Holy Church of God (1917); and United Pentecostal Church, International (1945). Oneness Pentecostals teach that the one true God, who has revealed himself as a Father, as a Son, and as Holy Spirit, is none other than Jesus Christ, in whom the fullness of the Godhead dwells bodily (Col. 2:9). As populist folk theologians, they usually forego, and even ignore, the work of systematic theology. In recent years, moreover, some have tried to sound more orthodox (most famously, T. D. Jakes). But in the main—and historically—they have denied the doctrine that God the Father and God the Holy Spirit possess complete personalities. More importantly (in their view), they insist that we should baptize in the name of Jesus only (in the manner of the book of Acts and the apostolic epistles) rather than in the trinitarian manner of Matthew 28.

21. Firm membership totals are hard to pin down for the AG, but generous estimates suggest a number well over fifteen million.

22. In recent years, scholars have labeled these churches "neo-charismatic," thus distinguishing them from charismatics resident in the mainline institutions.

23. Kenneth E. Hagin's (1917–2003) powerful "Word of Faith" movement is another good example of neo-charismatic influence.

Chapter 7

1. As discussed below, the neoevangelicals (or new evangelicals) are those who emerged from the doldrums of a defeated fundamentalism in the 1930s and 1940s, reengaging the broader culture with a proactive moral agenda.

2. Quoted in Robert J. Morgan, *Then Sings My Soul: 150 of the World's Greatest Hymn Stories* (Nashville: Thomas Nelson, 2003), 214–15.

3. Naturalism refers to a manner of thinking in which everything that happens is accounted for by means of natural causes (biochemical, social, or cultural), without recourse to the realm of supernatural agency. Modernism refers to a manner of thinking that favors modern (or recent) views and social trends over those of ancient times, requiring constant adaptation of traditional views and customs to contemporary standards.

4. Natural selection refers to the incremental reduction of genetic variations within a biological species, effecting a gradual transformation of that species into another that is better adapted to or suited for survival in its environment.

5. Today, most secular Bible scholars doubt the historicity of virtually *everything* in the Old Testament before the united kingdom of Saul, David, and Solomon.

6. Scholars distinguish "higher" biblical criticism from "lower" biblical criticism (also called textual criticism), which reconstructs the transmission of the biblical books themselves, comparing surviving manuscripts for the sake of establishing, or determining, the most reliable texts (i.e., those that best resemble what must have been the "original autographs").

7. Charles Augustus Briggs, *The Authority of Holy Scripture: An Inaugural Address*, 3rd ed. (New York: Charles Scribner's Sons, 1891), 35.

8. A. A. Hodge and B. B. Warfield, "Inspiration," in *The Princeton Theology, 1812–1921: Scripture, Science, and Theological Method from Archibald Alexander to Benjamin Warfield*, ed. Mark A. Noll (Grand Rapids: Baker Academic, 2001), 229–30.

9. This doctrine of the verbal inspiration of the Bible, sometimes referred to as "plenary [full or complete] verbal inspiration," has provided a safeguard for conservatives against the liberal tendency to separate the inner, essential meaning of biblical texts from their external, time-bound, expendable forms (i.e., the words and ancient worldviews, or mythology, of the Bible). For conservatives, the teachings of the Bible are inextricably connected to the language in and through which God revealed them. To abandon the words of Scripture is to render the Bible's meanings unintelligible or, worse, to open the door to fallible interpreters who would substitute their own words—and worldviews, or mythologies—for those that God inspired.

10. Hodge had followed Darwin's writings for years when, at the age of seventy-seven, he published his classic *What Is Darwinism?* (1874) (see Charles Hodge, "What Is Darwinism?" in *Princeton Theology*). In the book's conclusion, Hodge addressed his question summarily: "What is Darwinism? It is atheism. This does not mean, as before said, that Mr. Darwin himself and all who adopt his views are atheists; but it means that his theory is atheistic; that the exclusion of design from nature is . . . tantamount to atheism" (152).

11. H. Richard Niebuhr, *The Kingdom of God in America* (New York: Harper & Brothers, 1937), 193.

12. During the nineteenth century, boundaries between the postmillennial, premillennial, and amillennial views of the end times were drawn more clearly than ever before. Postmillennialists, who predominated the evangelical movement during its first several decades (up to the time of the Civil War), taught that Christ will return to earth *after* the golden millennial age (see Rev. 20), which will be ushered in with unprecedented revival and social improvement. Premillennialists, predominating the movement ever since, have taught that Christ will return to earth *before* the millennial age, inaugurating it personally and reigning on earth for a thousand years of peace and prosperity before the final judgment (many have viewed the thousand years symbolically, or approximately). Amillennialists, always a minority in the movement, teach a *spiritual* millennium, one in which Christ is said to be reigning now with the saints who are in heaven. (Amillennialists deny a literal, thousand-year interlude between the present history and judgment day.)

13. Dispensationalism is a special form of premillennialism that coalesced in England during the early nineteenth century. As designed by John Nelson

Darby (1800–1882), its founding architect who was also an early Plymouth Brethren leader, it divided all of history into seven "dispensations," six of which are centered around the progressive clarification of God's promises to the Jews. According to most dispensationalists, we are now in the sixth dispensation, a "great parenthesis" between the mainly Jewish dispensations, one that started with the birth of the Christian church at Pentecost and will continue until the eve of the great tribulation (Matt. 24:21; Rev. 6–19). During the current dispensation, God has turned from his chosen people (who rejected the promised Messiah) and has extended a plan of salvation to the Gentiles. In the great millennial age, or the seventh dispensation, God will resume his saving activity with the Jews. Although rooted in covenant theology, which dates from the Middle Ages, dispensationalism has two novel characteristics: a doctrine of the rapture (1 Thess. 4:17) of Christians out of the world before the great tribulation (and the seventh dispensation) and a division between New Testament texts that apply to national Israel (God's earthly people) and others that apply to the Christian church (God's heavenly people). It is a complicated system that has survived numerous changes during its brief, modern history. Its leading academic center is Dallas Theological Seminary (1924). Included among its proponents are D. L. Moody, William E. Blackstone (1841–1935), C. I. Scofield (1843–1921), Lewis Sperry Chafer (1871–1952), John F. Walvoord (1910–2002), and Charles C. Ryrie (1925–), who edited the dispensational *Ryrie Study Bible* (1976). Its best-known popular writers include Hal Lindsey (1929–), whose *Late Great Planet Earth* (1970) became the best-selling book in America for the decade of the 1970s, and Tim F. LaHaye (1926–) and Jerry B. Jenkins (1949–), whose Left Behind series of novels (1995–), which are premised on the doctrine of the church's rapture, has outsold Hal Lindsey's book by millions of copies.

14. Dwight L. Moody, "The Return of Our Lord," in *American Evangelicals, 1800–1900*, ed. William G. McLoughlin (New York: Harper & Row, 1968), 184–85.

15. Nondispensational, or historic, premillennialists (whose views date back to writings of the early church fathers) have usually not maintained such a low view of the culture and its potential for improvement (though they are less optimistic than postmillennialists).

16. The Westminster Confession (1647), which has always served as the primary doctrinal statement for Presbyterians, was revised in 1903 by northern Presbyterian leaders, both to accommodate progressives and to facilitate a merger with some of the (quasi-Arminian) Cumberland Presbyterians. The changes proved to be rather modest: A "Declaratory Statement" was added to explicate the text (especially chap. 3, on predestination); two new chapters were inserted (titled "Of the Holy Spirit" and "Of the Love of God, and Missions"); and three sections were modified (chaps. 16.7, 22.3, and 25.7). Taken together, these alterations stressed the *universal* scope of God's love and gospel call (at least his "external" call). They seemed to some to compromise the doctrine of limited atonement. But even the likes of B. B. Warfield, a solid Calvinist who was never soft on liberals or Arminians, gave the changes a public blessing: "The Revised Confession is . . . a Confession which every good Calvinist will recognize at once as his own" (Benjamin B. Warfield, *The Confession of Faith as Revised in 1903* [Richmond: Whittet & Shepperson, 1904], 39).

17. Quoted in Bill J. Leonard, ed., *The Dictionary of Baptists in America* (Downers Grove, IL: InterVarsity, 1994), 169.

18. Ibid., 292.

19. In American church history, second-degree separation dates from the time of Roger Williams (1603–83), the country's first Baptist preacher. However, fundamentalists have done the most to systematize the practice. It is separation not only from sin, worldliness, and apostasy (which all Christians advocate) but also from other Christians standing too close to these things (such as the Fundamentalist Fellowship).

20. A liberal Baptist layman and remarkable philanthropist, Rockefeller funded numerous people and institutions (such as Rauschenbusch and the Baptist University of Chicago) prior to Fosdick and his churches. In fact, Rockefeller had been the member at Park Avenue Baptist largely responsible for recruiting Fosdick in 1925. Before that, he had agreed to fund the distribution of Fosdick's sermon "Shall the Fundamentalists Win?" to the nation's Protestant clergy. Altogether, he gave well over thirty-two million dollars to the Riverside Church.

21. J. Gresham Machen, *Christianity and Liberalism* (New York: Macmillan, 1923), 7.

22. The change came under legal pressure from northern Presbyterians, who thought Presbyterian Church of America sounded too much like their own name, Presbyterian Church in the U.S.A. Note: The origin of today's Presbyterian Church *in* America (PCA), which has become a major force in the larger evangelical movement, is different from the origin of Machen's church. The PCA pulled out of the Presbyterian Church in the U.S. (or PCUS, a.k.a. the southern Presbyterian Church) late in 1973 over its recent liberalization. The PCUS later merged with the northern Presbyterian Church (1983), forming the Presbyterian Church (U.S.A.).

23. Quoted in Ned B. Stonehouse, *J. Gresham Machen: A Biographical Memoir* (Grand Rapids: Eerdmans, 1954), 310.

24. Rev. Harold John Ockenga (1905–85) of Boston's Park Street Church (as well as Fuller Seminary) likely coined this term in 1948. Long before that time, however, "new evangelicals" like him were representing a different brand of fundamentalism.

25. Carl F. H. Henry, *The Uneasy Conscience of Modern Fundamentalism* (Grand Rapids: Eerdmans, 1947), 18.

26. Ibid., 84.

27. During the early 1960s, Rev. Kenneth S. Kantzer (1917–2002) led Trinity into the suburbs of Chicago (Deerfield, Illinois). It had begun downtown as the Norwegian-Danish Department of Chicago Theological Seminary. For most of the twentieth century, it remained a tiny Bible school, serving the Scandinavian Pietists in the Evangelical Free Church of America (E.F.C.A., 1884). In the early 1960s, however, E.F.C.A. church officials decided to offer the school as a gift to the larger evangelical movement. Since that time, largely due to the ecumenical work of Kantzer, it has become one of the nation's largest seminaries.

28. *Christianity Today*, July 17, 1981, 26. See Douglas A. Sweeney, "Christianity Today," in *Popular Religious Magazines of the United States*, ed. P. Mark Fackler and Charles H. Lippy (Westport, CT: Greenwood Press, 1995), 144–51.

29. *Christianity Today*, October 15, 1956, 20.

30. During the 1950s, the number of church members in America grew from 64.5 million to 114.5 million. By 1960, more than 60 percent of the nation belonged to a church.

31. The mainline Protestant Council of the City of New York sponsored the New York City crusade. This was new to Graham's evangelistic ministry in the United States, but it was not unprecedented. Three years earlier (1954), Graham had won the support of moderates and liberals for his greater London crusade (held at the Harringay arena), alarming numerous evangelicals in Britain.

32. Significantly, their spiritual descendants would reengage American politics in the 1970s, erecting what is now called the New Christian Right. Drawn back into the culture wars by the drastic liberalization of the nation's family values (particularly those that pertained to sex and reproductive rights), leaders such as Jerry Falwell (1933–), Pat Robertson, and Tim and Bev (1929–) LaHaye would make a dent in local and regional politics—and Republican conventions—through grassroots organizations such as the Moral Majority (1979), the Christian Coalition (1989), Concerned Women for America (1979), and the American Coalition for Traditional Values (1984).

33. There were many supporters of Graham—and of neoevangelicalism—with little history at all in fundamentalism. Important examples include Henry, who was converted from virtual paganism in early adulthood (1933), and Kenneth Kantzer, who was raised within a nominal Lutheran home but dated his evangelical faith to a collegiate conversion (1935). Such people affirmed the fundamentalists' passion for theological orthodoxy but recoiled from its militancy and separatism.

34. See also the works suggested in chapter 1.

Conclusion

1. In recent decades, several Southern Baptist leaders have debated whether to refer to themselves as evangelicals. The vast majority think they should, but some prefer to stand apart, defining themselves more narrowly in Southern Baptist terms. See James Leo Garrett Jr., E. Glenn Hinson, and James E. Tull, *Are Southern Baptists "Evangelicals"?* (Macon, GA: Mercer University Press, 1983).

2. These critics are working in the tradition of confessional Protestant churches that have always been ambivalent about the evangelical movement, particularly the Lutheran Church-Missouri Synod (LCMS, 1847) and the Christian Reformed Church in North America (CRC, 1857). These groups have lingered for more than a century on the margins of evangelicalism, even as they have embraced other forms of American culture. They respect evangelicals' concerns for Protestant orthodoxy but hesitate to enter into the eighteenth-century twist. Fearing the doctrinal and practical effects of its ecumenism—especially with groups that trust too much in spiritual emotions—they have affiliated often on an ad hoc basis without immersing themselves in the movement as a whole.

3. Latin Americans and Asians have inhabited the United States since long before 1965, but the Immigration Act opened the door to rapid growth in both their numbers and civil rights. On the new immigration generally, see R. Stephen Warner and Judith G. Wittner, eds., *Gatherings in Diaspora: Religious Communities and the New Immigration* (Philadelphia: Temple University Press, 1998).

4. On Hispanic evangelicals, see Gastón Espinosa, Virgilio Elizondo, and Jesse Miranda, "Hispanic Churches in American Public Life: Summary of Findings," *Interim Reports* (March 2003), Institute for Latino Studies, University of Notre Dame. As reported in this summary, the Pew Charitable Trusts has funded a scientific survey of 2,310 Hispanics (93 percent of whom identified themselves as Christians—70 percent as Catholics, 23 percent as Protestants). Extrapolating from the survey data, Espinosa and his colleagues suggest that there are approximately 6.6 million born-again Hispanics in the United States today, that "the Latino religious marketplace is . . . increasingly Evangelical, Pentecostal, and Charismatic" (22), and that younger Hispanics (second- and third-generation Americans), especially, are turning to evangelicalism. "To put these findings in national perspective, there are now more Latino Protestants in the United States [mostly evangelical] than Jews or Muslims or Episcopalians and Presbyterians combined" (16). The best book on a major subset of Hispanic evangelicals is Arlene M. Sánchez Walsh, *Latino Pentecostal Identity: Evangelical Faith, Self, and Society* (New York: Columbia University Press, 2003). See also Gastón Espinosa, Virgilio Elizondo, and Jesse Miranda, eds., *Latino Religions and Civic Activism in the United States* (New York: Oxford University Press, forthcoming); and idem, *Latino Religions and Politics in American Public Life* (New York: Oxford University Press, forthcoming).

5. For statistical information on Asian American Christianity, see the forthcoming project, "Asian and Pacific Islander American Religious Leadership Today: The Report of the API Pulpit and Pew Project (2004)," directed by Timothy Tseng (with the help of eleven other Asian American research scholars) and funded by the Lilly Endowment. See also Tony Carnes and Fenggang Yang, eds., *Asian American Religions: The Making and Remaking of Borders and Boundaries* (New York: New York University Press, 2004). The authors note the profound religiosity of most Asian Americans and their disproportionate contributions to evangelicalism.

Index